TEXT: ALEXA POORTIER
PHOTOS: RETO GUNTLI & AGI SIMOES

This must be Paradise

**CONSCIOUS
TRAVEL INSPIRATIONS**

teNeues

Contents
Inhaltsverzeichnis

INTRODUCTION	4	BAMBU INDAH, BALI	79
SONEVA KIRI, THAILAND	7	THE LEGIAN SEMINYAK, BALI, INDONESIA	89
SONEVA JANI, MALDIVES	15	THE LEGIAN SIRE, LOMBOK, INDONESIA	97
SONEVA FUSHI, MALDIVES	25	SONG SAA, CAMBODIA	105
JOALI BEING, MALDIVES	33	FOUR SEASONS THE NAM HAI, VIETNAM	115
FOUR SEASONS LANDAA GIRAAVARU, MALDIVES	45	GENGHIS KHAN RETREAT, MONGOLIA	125
THE DATAI, MALAYSIA	55	PUSHKAR CAMEL FAIR, INDIA	137
BAWAH RESERVE, INDONESIA	67	ADRERE AMELLAL, EGYPT	147

KASBAH DE TOUBKAL, MOROCCO	157	THE ALPINA GSTAAD, SWITZERLAND	235
MANOR HOUSES, PORTUGAL	165	BERGHUUS RADONS, SWITZERLAND	247
FINCA SERENA, SPAIN	175	BIOS	254
COQUILLADE PROVENCE RESORT & SPA, FRANCE	183	SUSTAINABILITY ALLIANCE, PROGRAMS AND CERTIFICATION	255
THE TORRIDON, SCOTLAND	195	IMPRINT	256
WHATLEY MANOR, ENGLAND	205		
HOTEL PALAFITTE, SWITZERLAND	215		
BEAU RIVAGE PALACE, LAUSANNE, SWITZERLAND	223		

Introduction

Einleitung

Travel is one of our greatest joys because of the way it makes us feel when we retreat or seek adventure, when we relate with different people and immerse in their cultures, and when we witness nature's immense beauty, and its magic enhances our lives. Tourism's positive impacts are brilliant. It's a global driver of economic prosperity and employment, redistributes wealth, finances infrastructure, and supports conservation. It can promote goodwill and respect of culture, heritage, and traditions. In tandem with its growth, tourism's negative impacts are massive and alarming. Jobs are often poorly paid and seasonal, and tourism revenue often leaks out to foreign companies. Over-tourism deteriorated the quality of life in popular places, overused resources, and increased congestion, consumption, cost of living, cultural clashes, pollution, and waste. Many degraded their natural and cultural landscapes. Loss of native customs and traditions, substance abuse, and sex exploitation can occur.

In 1987, a concerned United Nations (UN) introduced a sustainable development concept that meets the needs of the present without compromising the ability of future generations to meet their own needs. A few tourism vanguards became Guardians of places, while others did little to nothing for decades. Travel and tourism contribute to climate emergencies, emitting a disturbing 11% of global greenhouse gas (GHG) emissions pre-covid, with half from transport. EV charging networks and Sustainable Aviation Fuel (SAF) need to scale. SAF blending, a lighter load, less waste, a non-stop flight, and offsetting can reduce aviation emissions today.

Changing consumer attitudes on sustainability prompted more tourism operators to seek certifications. Over 400 certification schemes and big hotel groups offer programs ranging from rigorous science-based to easy self-reporting, but without regulations, the ocean of labels has become an ocean of confusion and greenwash (misleading 'green' messages with no proof, for profit), resulting in a crisis of trust. By 2021, surveys revealed over 80% of travelers think sustainable travel is vital, but the willingness to pay for sustainable products and services vary across generations and countries. To fight greenwashing, Google Travel's Eco-Certified label differentiate hotels with qualified certifications and 3rd party expert audits. Other Online Travel Agents identify sustainability practices and give badges/labels. The 2022 UN Climate Report warned that rising GHG emissions must peak before 2025 worldwide plus drop by 48% by 2030 including methane by 1/3 to try to limit warming to 1.5°C (34.7°F), the red line for climate breakdown. Solutions exist but the gap between Net Zero pledges and reality is vast.

Reisen ist eine unserer größten Freuden, weil es uns gefühlsmäßig bewegt, wenn wir Abgeschiedenheit oder Abenteuer suchen, andere Menschen und Kulturen hautnah erleben und Zeuge der unendlichen Schönheit der Natur werden, und die Magie des Reisens bereichert unser Leben. Tourismus ist ein wunderbarer Katalysator des Guten. Er ist globaler Konjunkturmotor, verteilt Reichtum um, finanziert Infrastruktur und unterstützt den Naturschutz. Er kann den wohlwollenden Respekt vor Kulturerbe und Traditionen fördern. Parallel zu seinem Wachstum sind die negativen Auswirkungen massiv und besorgniserregend. Jobs sind oft schlecht bezahlt und saisonabhängig, Tourismuseinnahmen fließen oft an ausländische Unternehmen. Overtourism, also ein „Zuviel" an Tourismus, hat die Lebensqualität an beliebten Orten verschlechtert, Ressourcen erschöpft und für mehr Staus, Konsum, Lebenshaltungskosten, kulturelle Konflikte, Umweltverschmutzung und Müll gesorgt. Vielerorts verkommen Natur- und Kulturlandschaften. Brauchtum und Tradition können verloren gehen, auch Drogenmissbrauch und sexuelle Ausbeutung kommen vor.

1987 legte die besorgte UNO ein nachhaltiges Entwicklungskonzept auf, das den Bedürfnissen der Gegenwart genügt, ohne künftige Generationen zu beeinträchtigen. Einige Tourismusvordenker wurden zu Bewahrern von Orten, während andere jahrzehntelang wenig bis nichts taten. Reisen und Tourismus tragen zu Klimakrisen bei. Vor Corona lag der CO_2-Ausstoß bei beunruhigenden 11 Prozent der globalen Treibhausgasemissionen (THG), die Hälfte davon verkehrsbedingt. Das Ladestationsnetzwerk für Elektroautos und nachhaltiger Flugzeugtreibstoff (SAF) müssen dimensioniert werden. Die 50:50-Mischung aus Kerosin und klimaneutralem Kraftstoff (SAF), weniger Ladegewicht und Müll, Direktflüge und CO_2-Kompensationszahlungen können heute die Emissionen reduzieren. Die veränderten Einstellungen der Verbraucher veranlassten mehr Tourismusunternehmen, sich um Nachhaltigkeitszertifizierungen zu bemühen. Über 400 Zertifizierungssysteme und große Hotelketten bieten Programme an, die von streng wissenschaftlichen bis hin zu einfachen Selbstauskünften reichen; mit der Zertifikatsschwemme nimmt aber auch täuschendes Greenwashing exponentiell zu, was zu einer Vertrauenskrise führt.

Bis 2021 halten Umfragen zufolge über 80 Prozent nachhaltiges Reisen für lebenswichtig, aber die Bereitschaft, für klimaneutrale Produkte und Dienstleistungen zu bezahlen, ist von Generation zu Generation und von Land zu Land unterschiedlich. Um Greenwashing zu bekämpfen, differenziert das Ökolabel von Google Travel Hotels mit qualifizierten Zertifizierungen und Prüfungen durch

At this most urgent of times, it is vital for Travel and Tourism owners and operators to take responsibility for their total impacts on communities and the environment, contribute to conservation and aim for Net Zero emissions or better this decade. Extravagant and wasteful destinations need to transform to be a collective community with purpose, where wisdom is gained from nature and where visitors can experience joy and their humanity.

Sustainable places to stay with accountability and transparency have courageous leaders who value trust and use the power of business to achieve the UN Global Goals, measure their total impacts, and reduce plus offset their carbon footprint. They share actionable knowledge to replenish and regenerate, advance circularity, and provide comfort and service in a responsible way. They care for their community, hire locals first, train to hone vocation and life-skills, and support local suppliers with shared values. They offer authentic experiences that create happiness and meaningful connections that engage with local life and nature.

This book spotlights 25 delightful properties and their leaders with purpose at different levels in their sustainability journey. They are inspired to show progress, oppose greenwash and aim to be 'the best for our world'.

What can travelers do?

True sustainable travel is magical, minimises negative impacts and leaves a destination better than we find it. **Be aware of your wallet's power** and ask where your money is going. Make informed decisions. **Decarbonize your travel**. Take an eVehicle or train for short trips under 500km. Choose a non-stop, economy flight for long haul and offset emissions. Fly less and stay longer, prioritising support for sustainable, certified, and audited hotels and tourism operators. Pack light and bring reusables, eco toiletries and solar chargers. Walk, cycle, paddle, or sail. Choose locally grown and sustainably sourced food and spa products. Waste less, go paperless and refuse single-use plastic. Limit digital use and detox. **Respect nature, people, and cultures**. Tread lightly. Support local guides and immerse in a destination's history, life, and culture. Pay fairly for purchases that benefit local craftspeople. **Protect wildlife**. Avoid zoos, animal shows, dubious safaris and refuse endangered animal products. Be curious and look, but do not feed, ride, touch, toxify or pet them. **Give and volunteer the right way** through reputable charities. **Activate your radar for greenwash** and speak up for better travel!

Drittexperten. Andere Online-Reisebüros vergeben je nach Einhaltung von Kriterien Badges bzw. Labels. Der UN-Klimabericht 2022 mahnte, dass steigende CO_2-Emissionen vor 2025 weltweit ihren Höhepunkt erreichen und bis 2030 um 48 Prozent sinken müssen, um die 1,5-Grad-Grenze nicht zu überschreiten. Es gibt Lösungen, aber zwischen dem Netto-Null-Versprechen und der Realität herrscht eine tiefe Kluft. In diesen Zeiten akuter Bedrängnis ist es für alle Player der Reisebranche von entscheidender Bedeutung, die Verantwortung für ihren sozio-ökologischen Impact zu übernehmen und in diesem Jahrzehnt mit Netto-Null-Emissionen oder noch besser abzuschneiden.

Unterkünfte mit Nachhaltigkeitsanspruch, Verantwortungsbewusstsein und Transparenz haben mutige Führungskräfte, die Wert auf Vertrauen legen und die unternehmerische Power nutzen, um die globalen UN-Ziele erreichen. Es sind Entrepreneure, die ihre Gesamtauswirkungen messen und ihren CO_2-Fußabdruck reduzieren. Sie teilen umsetzbares Wissen, um verbrauchte Ressourcen wieder aufzufüllen und zu regenerieren, fördern den Wirtschaftskreislauf und bieten auf verantwortungsvolle Weise Komfort und Service. Sie sorgen für das örtliche Gemeinwohl, stellen vorzugsweise Einheimische ein, bilden Talente und Lebenskompetenzen aus und holen lokale Zulieferer mit gemeinsamen Werten mit ins Boot. Sie bieten authentische Erlebnisse, die Glück und sinnvolle Verbindungen schaffen, um sich mit dem Leben und der Natur vor Ort zu befcssen. Dieses Buch präsentiert 25 bezaubernde Anwesen und ihre Visionäre, die auf verschiedenen Ebenen ihren Weg der Nachhaltigkeit gehen.

Was können Reisende tun?

Wirklich nachhaltiges Reisen ist voller Magie, minimiert negative Auswirkungen und hinterlässt eine Destination besser, als wir sie vorfinden. **Machen Sie sich die Macht Ihres Portemonnaies bewusst**. Fragen Sie, wohin Ihr Geld fließt. Treffen Sie fundierte Entscheidungen. **Dekarbonisieren Sie Ihre Reise**. Nehmen Sie für Kurzstrecken unter 500 km ein Elektroauto oder den Zug. Wählen Sie einen Economy-Direktflug für Langstrecken und kompensieren Sie CO_2-Emissionen. Fliegen Sie weniger, bleiben Sie länger und geben Sie nachhaltigen, zertifizierten und geprüften Hotels und Tourismusunternehmen den Vorrang. Reisen Sie mit leichtem Gepäck und nehmen Sie wiederverwendbare Produkte, Öko-Toilettenartikel und Solarladegeräte mit. Wandern, radeln, paddeln oder segeln Sie. Wählen Sie Slowfood und nachhaltige Spa-Produkte aus der Region. Produzieren Sie weniger Müll, stellen Sie auf papierlos um und lehnen Sie Einwegplastik ab. Schränken Sie Ihre Bildschirmzeit ein und machen Sie eine Digital-Detox-Kur. **Respektieren Sie die Natur und begegnen Sie Menschen und Kulturen mit entsprechendem Taktgefühl**. Unterstützen Sie lokale Guides und tauchen Sie ein in die Geschichte, das Leben und die Kultur einer Destination. Kaufen Sie Fair-Produkte, was dem lokalen Kunsthandwerk zugutekommt. **Schützen Sie wild lebende Tiere**. Vermeiden Sie Zoos, Tiershows, dubiose Safaris und lehnen Sie Produkte von gefährdeten Tieren ab. Seien Sie neugierig und beobachten Sie die Tiere – nicht füttern, reiten, berühren, vergiften oder streicheln! **Leisten Sie Freiwilligenarbeit oder eine Spende** für wohltätige Zwecke über anerkannte karitative Organisationen. **Entwickeln Sie ein Gespür für Greenwashing** und setzen Sie sich für ein besseres Reisen ein!

SONEVA KIRI, THAILAND

Fall In Love With Nature

Soneva is a creator of sustainable and luxurious resorts in Thailand and the Maldives where the sun is glorious and shines for more than 2,000 hours a year. Soneva Kiri is surrounded by lush rainforest and white beaches on Koh Kood Island in the Gulf of Thailand, a shallow inlet in the South China Sea. Soneva Fushi is nestled in the pristine Baa Atoll UNESCO Biosphere Reserve on Kunfunadhoo Island and Soneva Jani is surrounded by a private lagoon in the Noonu Atoll on Medhufaru Island.

Soneva is an amalgam of the founder's names - Sonu and Eva. It is a story of two people in love, who fell in love with the nature in these pristine islands, where their thriving community works hand in hand with nature to craft bespoke experiences and transformative wellness. They believe that if people are inspired to love nature, then we are more likely to protect it.

Sonu and Eva Shivdasani are the guardians of places that existed long before them. The fabulously formidable Eva, whose Swedish parents brought her up thinking of the planet, was fondly nicknamed 'The Conscience' by their team, for she ensured that everything they build is both sustainable and ethical. Inspired by nature's magnitude, mystery and enchanting beauty, sustainability has run through the heart of Soneva since they launched their first resort in 1995. Committed to exist in harmony with their natural environment, they pledged to protect the biodiversity and habitats on and around their resorts. They support local communities, local suppliers and hire locally when available; beyond that, they nurture their host's strengths, encourage lifelong learning, and inspire a love of the ocean and the local environment through water sports, education, and community outreach activities.

Soneva's core purpose is imaginative and enlightening Slow Life and offers guests luxuries that enhance their health whilst minimizing their impact on the environment. The Soneva Stars programme highlights Michelin-starred chefs, sporting legends and acclaimed therapists. Their inspiring festivals bring literary and cultural events to

Soneva ist Gründer von nachhaltigen Eco-Luxury-Resorts auf den Malediven und in Thailand. Mit rund 1.190 Koralleninseln im Indischen Ozean, umgeben von weißpudrigem Sand und kristallklarem, azurblauem Wasser, lockt das Malediven-Archipel mit tropischem Klima und mehr als 2.700 Sonnenstunden pro Jahr. Das Soneva Fushi liegt im Baa Atoll, einem unberührten UNESCO-Biosphärenreservat auf der Insel Kunfunadhoo, das Soneva Jani ist von einer Privatlagune auf der Insel Medhufaru im Noonu-Atoll umgeben. Das Soneva Kiri liegt in einem üppigen Regenwald versteckt und lockt mit weißen Sandstränden auf der Insel Koh Kood im Golf von Thailand, einer flachen Bucht im Südchinesischen Meer.

Soneva setzt sich zusammen aus den Vornamen des Gründerduos Sonu und Eva (Shivdasani). Es ist die Geschichte eines Traumpaares, das sich in die Natur dieser jungfräulichen Inseln verliebt hat. Ihre prosperierende Ortsgemeinde arbeitet Hand in Hand mit der Natur, um individuell zugeschnittene Experiences und transformative Wellness zu gestalten. Sie glauben, dass wir die Natur eher schützen, wenn Menschen dazu inspiriert werden, sie zu lieben.

Sonu und Eva Shivdasani sind die Bewahrer von Orten, die es schon lange vor ihnen gab. Die bewundernswerte Eva, deren schwedische Eltern ihr die Liebe zum Planeten vermittelt haben, wird von ihrem Team liebevoll „The Conscience" genannt; denn bei allem, was gebaut wird, hat sie für Nachhaltigkeit und Einhaltung der Umweltethik gesorgt. Inspiriert von der Größe, dem Geheimnis und der bezaubernden Schönheit der Natur, liegt ihr seit Eröffnung ihres ersten Resorts im Jahr 1995 die Umweltverträglichkeit am Herzen. Getreu ihrem Credo, in Harmonie mit ihrem natürlichen Umfeld zu leben und die Artenvielfalt und Habitate in und um ihre Resorts herum zu schützen, unterstützen sie die örtliche Ökonomie und stellen nach Möglichkeit auch Locals ein. Darüber hinaus fördern sie die Stärken ihrer (einheimischen) Gastgeber und Guides durch Lifelong Learning, wecken die Liebe zum Meer und zur unmittelbaren Umgebung durch Wassersport, Bildung und Einbindung der Ortsgemeinschaft.

Nestle within lush tropical rainforest and choose to stay at Soneva Kiri's sprawling Beach Pool Reserve villas perched atop cliffs or Beach Pool Suites on the sandy shore. Relax and enjoy dining experiences with stunning views across the Gulf of Thailand.

Inmitten des üppigen tropischen Regenwaldes können Sie in den Beach Pool-Villen des Soneva Kiri auf den Klippen oder in den Beach Pool-Suiten am Sandstrand wohnen. Entspannen Sie sich und genießen Sie kulinarische Erlebnisse mit atemberaubendem Blick auf den Golf von Thailand.

Villas with private pools and outdoor shower. Soneva Kiri Spa offers intuitive therapies and massages from around the world including Abhyangam ancient Indian, Thai, Swedish and Deep Tissue. Be hoisted above treetops for a surprising dining experience.

Die Villen verfügen über private Pools und Außendusche. Das Soneva Kiri Spa bietet intuitive Therapien und Massagen aus aller Welt, darunter Abhyangam, altindisch, thailändisch, schwedisch und Deep Tissue. Lassen Sie sich für ein überraschendes kulinarisches Erlebnis über die Baumkronen heben.

SONEVA JANI, MALDIVES

life; in addition, there are wellness innovations and gastronomy with a lively, global flair.

Nature has inspired Soneva's barefoot architecture, its down-to-earth personality, its 'no news, no shoes' philosophy, and its innovation to Reducing, Recycling and Inspiring. They are radically reducing the volume of plastic arriving on the islands, responsibly dispose of waste, and reuse or recycle 90% of their waste. They initiated a waste management project – Soneva Namoona – in January 2019 in partnership with their neighbouring islands. Drinking water is bottled on site in re-usable glass and revenues from its sale go to the Soneva Foundation to fund the work of charities such as Water Charity and Thirst Aid. They are regenerative and each Soneva resort features an Eco Waste-to-Wealth Centre, lush organic gardens, for instance, are irrigated by grey water and nurtured by compost from the resort kitchens.

The Soneva organisation and all their resorts are 100% carbon neutral since 2012. This is made possible by introducing a 2% environmental levy on all guest stays since 2008, funding Soneva Foundation which invests into programs that have a positive environmental, social and economic impact. Soneva Ocean Stewards successfully tackles marine protection issues. Slow Life Symposium, Clean Water Projects, Soneva Water benefit the community. Action Against Hunger, Care for Children create long-term economic benefits. Myanmar Stoves Campaign and Soneva Forest Restoration Project provide the carbon credits to offset carbon emissions.

Soneva and its founders are pioneers of sustainable luxury in the hospitality industry since 1995 and they are committed to leading the fight against climate change within the tourism sector. Focused on action, they have partnered with Swiss organisation Coralive.org to work on a coral propagation project, the Maldives' largest coral nursery. Their ambitious plans aim at harvesting 50,000 coral fragments every year to restore and renew the reef systems.

As a strong advocate of the overall positive impact of travel and tourism, Soneva's founders believe that luxury, including travel, and sustainability must go hand in hand, and that hoteliers and owners must be a positive force for change. Looking to the future, for this industry to survive in a post-COVID era, they believe it will be vital for travel and tourism to have a net positive contribution to conservation, the environment, as well as the community.

Kernziel von Soneva ist ein fantasievolles, bewusstseinsveränderndes SLOW LIFE mit Luxury-Angeboten für mehr Gesundheit, jedoch zugleich mit positivem Impact auf die Umwelt. Publikumsmagneten ihres Soneva Stars-Programms sind Michelin-Sterneköche, Sportlegenden und anerkannte Gesundheitscoaches. Ihre inspirierenden Feste erfüllen Literatur und Kultur mit Leben; zusätzliche gibt es Wellness-Innovationen und eine Gastronomie mit lebendigem, globalem Flair. Auch Sonevas Barfuß-Architektur steht ganz im Zeichen der Natur: Der bodenständige Charakter, das Motto „no news, no shoes" und der Trend zum Reduzieren, Recyceln und Inspirieren sind Teil der Innovation. Das tourismusbedingte Plastikaufkommen wird drastisch reduziert, Müll wird verantwortungsbewusst entsorgt und 90 Prozent des Abfalls werden wiederverwertet oder recycelt. Auf ihre Initiative hin wurde im Januar 2019 in Kooperation mit den benachbarten Inseln das Abfallmanagementprojekt "Soneva Namoona" ins Leben gerufen: Trinkwasser wird vor Ort in wiederverwendbare Glasflaschen abgefüllt und die Einnahmen aus dem Verkauf gehen an die Soneva Foundation, um Wohlfahrtsverbände wie Water Charity und Thirst Aid zu fördern. Die Betreiber wirtschaften regenerativ, d.h. jedes Soneva-Resort verfügt über eine "Waste-to-Wealth"-Zentrale für lückenloses Recycling.

Soneva und alle seine Resorts sind seit 2012 100 % klimaneutral. Ermöglicht wird dies durch die 2008 eingeführte Umweltabgabe von 2 % des Aufenthaltspreises. Finanziert wird das Ganze von der Soneva-Stiftung, die in Programme mit positivem Impact auf Umwelt, Gesellschaft und Wirtschaft investiert. Soneva Ocean Stewards engagiert sich erfolgreich für den Meeresschutz. Initiativen wie das Slow-Life-Symposium, Clean Water Projects, Soneva Water kommen dem Gemeinwesen zugute. Maßnahmen gegen Hunger und Kinderfürsorge schaffen langfristig volkswirtschaftlichen Nutzen. Mit zertifizierten Kohlenstoffprojekten wie dem Myanmar Stoves Campaign, einer Aktion für brennstoffeffiziente Kocher, und dem Soneva-Aufforstungsprojekt werden CO_2-Emissionen kompensiert.

Soneva und seine Gründer sind seit 1995 Pioniere des nachhaltigen Luxus in der Hotellerie und nehmen im Kampf gegen den Klimawandel in der Tourismusbranche eine Vorreiterrolle ein. Maßnahmenfokussiert hat sich Soneva mit der schweizerischen Organisation Coralive.org zusammengetan, um die größte Korallengärtnerei der Malediven in ihrer Arbeit zu unterstützen. Das ambitionierte Vorhaben hat sich zum Ziel gesetzt, jedes Jahr 50.000 abgebrochene Korallenfragmente zu sammeln, um die Riffsysteme zu restaurieren. Als starker Befürworter des insgesamt positiven Impacts des Tourismus glauben die Soneva-Gründer, dass Luxury-Angebote – auch im Reisesegment – mit Nachhaltigkeit einhergehen sollten, und dass Hoteliers und Eigentümer die treibende Kraft für den Wandel sein müssen. Mit Blick auf die Zukunft wird es für den Fortbestand dieser Branche in einer Post-Covid-Ära aus ihrer Sicht von entscheidender Bedeutung sein, dass Reisen einen positiven Nettobeitrag zum Naturschutz, zur Umwelt und zum Gemeinwesen leistet.

Soneva Jani offers Water and Island Retreats with private pools, unforgettable views, vast space, privacy, and most feature waterslides into the lagoon and a retractable roof.

Page 16-17: Ride a bamboo bike across the wooden boardwalk that connects two islands.

Soneva Jani bietet Wasser- und Insel-Retreats mit privaten Pools, unvergesslichen Ausblicken, viel Platz und Privatsphäre. Die meisten verfügen über Wasserrutschen in die Lagune und ein einziehbares Dach.

Seite 16-17: Fahren Sie mit einem Bambusfahrrad über die Holzpromenade, die zwei Inseln miteinander verbindet.

Sunbathe on a hammock over the lagoon. Experience the Crab Shack for Sri Lankan Mud Crab curry, the Director's Cut for Japanese cuisine and a movie, and the observatory deck for a crafted menu and be starstruck. Plant corals with resident Marine biologists.

Nehmen Sie ein Sonnenbad in einer Hängematte über der Lagune. Lassen Sie sich im Crab Shack mit Mud-Crab-Curry aus Sri Lanka verwöhnen, genießen Sie im Director's Cut japanische Spitzenküche oder auf der Beobachtungsplattform einen Film und ein dazugehöriges Menü. Des Abends können Sie von hier die Sterne bestaunen. Mit den ansässigen Meeresbiologen können Sie Korallen züchten.

SONEVA FUSHI, MALDIVES

Villas have vast living spaces with pools and ocean views. Boardwalk leads to 'Out of the Blue' offering Vietnamese, Japanese, Indonesian and grill dining outlets.

Page 26-27: 'Fresh in the Garden' rooftop restaurant overlooks stunning views, and 8 Water Retreats with a pool and water slide.

Die Villen haben große Wohnbereiche mit Pools und Meerblick. Der Holzsteg führt zum "Out of the Blue", in dem vietnamesische, japanische und indonesische Grillgerichte angeboten werden.

Seite 26-27: Das "Fresh in the Garden"-Restaurant bietet einen atemberaubenden Ausblick und 8 Water Retreats samt Pool und Wasserrutsche.

A hot glass studio recycles used glass to create bespoke glassware and striking works of art for the villas and restaurants. Metal waste is recycled to create ornaments. Learn about permaculture, the multi-use for coconuts, and pick greens and herbs for your lunch at Eco Centro and organic gardens.

In einer Werkstatt wird Altglas recycelt, um maßgefertigte Glaswaren und beeindruckende Kunstwerke für die Villen und Restaurants herzustellen. Metallabfälle werden ebenso für die Herstellung von Ornamenten recycelt. Erfahren Sie mehr über Permakultur, die vielen Verwendungszwecke von Kokosnüssen und pflücken Sie Gemüse und Kräuter für Ihr Mittagessen im Eco Centro und seinen Gärten.

JOALI BEING, MALDIVES

Weightless Renewal

On the secluded Bodufushi Island of Raa Atoll in northern Maldives, Joali Wellbeing is a luxurious and sensory biophilic space embraced by lush coconut palms, pristine beaches, and an azure blue lagoon. A conscious GM Özgür Cengiz leads a team of naturopaths, therapists, movement specialists, nutritionists, and biologists from 35 countries and a 50% Maldavian staff with a shared purpose to have a positive impact on their guests and community focused on healthy basics and nature.

To achieve a sense of 'weightlessness', Joali offers an immersive program that harnesses science, technology and knowledge to rebalance the four pillars of wellbeing - mind, skin, microbiome and energy. The transformation journey is personalised for each guest's lifestyle and goal, aiming to enhance a deeper connection with the body, mind and nature with a blend of ancient and modern methods, guided learning and a delicious range of healthy cuisine. They can join activities in nature with resident biologists working on coral farms and sea turtle habitats, with gardeners working in organic gardens, and join the resort team in meetings with suppliers and beach cleaning with the community.

Joali supports community needs through a local council, works with local suppliers, and shares the joy of wellness and actionable knowledge with local ladies through culinary classes, with local schools, and with primary students invited for a fun day at Joali. They use smart technology to control energy, water and waste, and offer curious guests weekly tours for a back-of-the-house insight of their positive actions.

Auf der abgelegenen Insel Bodufushi im Raa-Atoll im Norden der Malediven ist das Joali Being ein luxuriöser, lebensfreundlicher Ort mit allem, was die Sinne betört: üppige Kokospalmen, unberührte Strände und eine azurblaue Lagune. Der souveräne Geschäftsführer Özgür Cengiz leitet ein naturheilkundliches Team aus wissenschaftlich qualifizierten Bewegungs- und Ernährungscoaches und Biologen aus 35 Ländern, wobei die Hälfte des Personals aus Locals besteht. Ihr gemeinsames Ziel ist es, ihre Gäste und die Ortsgemeinschaft zu einem gesunden, naturnahen Lebensstil zurückzuführen.

Um Regeneration und ein Gefühl der „Schwerelosigkeit" zu erreichen, bietet Joali ein umfassendes Wellbeing-Programm an, das Wissenschaft, Technik und Wissen nutzt, um die vier Säulen des Wohlbefindens – Geist, Haut, Mikrobiom und Energie – wieder ins Gleichgewicht zu bringen. Die Transformationsreise ist individuell zugeschnitten, je nach Lebensstil und Ziel eines jeden Gastes, und will eine tiefere Verbindung mit Körper, Geist und Natur schaffen. Erreicht werden soll dies mit einer Mischung aus altem Wissen und moderner Medizin, angeleitetem Lernen und vielfältigen gesunden Gaumenfreuden. Die Gäste können in wissenschaftlicher Begleitung Korallenfarmen und Meeresschildkrötenhabitate erkunden, sich durch Biogärten führen lassen, an Resort-Meetings mit lokalen Lieferanten teilnehmen und bei Strandreinigungsaktionen mitmachen.

Joali unterstützt die kommunalen Bedürfnisse durch einen Gemeinderat, arbeitet mit Locals zusammen und teilt die Freude am Wohlbefinden und anwendbares Wissen der einheimischen Frauen im Rahmen von Kochkursen, und auch mit Grundschulklassen, die zu einem Fun Day ins Joali eingeladen werden. Das Resort nutzt smarte Technologie für kontrolliertes Energie-, Wasser- und Abfallmanagement und bietet neugierigen Gästen bei wöchentlichen Führungen einen Blick hinter die Kulissen ihres Engagements.

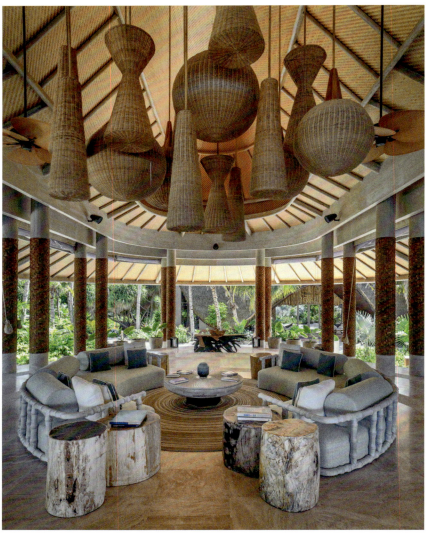

The resort's biophilic design by Autoban emerged from the idea of weightlessness that increases connectivity to the natural environment in the curved jetty lounge, the ocean pool and beach villas, beach sanctuary, dining spaces and wellness centre.

Das biophile Design des Resorts vom Designstudio Autoban entstand aus einer Idee der Schwerelosigkeit, die die Verbindung zur natürlichen Umgebung – in der geschwungenen Steg-Lounge, dem Meerespool und den Strandvillen, dem Beach Sanctuary, den Speiseräumen und dem Wellness-Center – verstärkt.

The spectacular jetty at sunset. The Areka Wellness Centre interior lounge, Kashi hydrotherapy hall leading to treatment rooms and Aktar Herbology Centre is set amidst breath-taking gardens and seaside vistas.

Page 40-41: The path leading to Areka Wellness Centre.

Der spektakuläre Steg bei Sonnenuntergang. Die Interior-Lounge des Wellness-Zentrums Areka, die Hydrotherapie-Halle Kashi führen zu den Behandlungsräumen und dem Kräuterkunden-Zentrum Aktar, welches inmitten eines atemberaubenden Gartens und mit Blick aufs Meer gelegen ist.

Seite 40-41: Der Pfad, der zum Wellness-Zentrum Areka führt.

FOUR SEASONS LANDAA GIRAAVARU, MALDIVES

The Island Of Shifting Sands

The Baa Atoll Biosphere Reserve comprises 75 islands in the Maldives and supports one of the largest groups of coral reefs in the Indian Ocean. Landaa Giraavaru is a protected 44-acre island wilderness at Baa Atoll with the luxurious Four Seasons Resort surrounded by white sandy beaches and turquoise lagoons. A passionate GM Armando Kraenzlin and an energised team are heartened to cultivate connection and appreciation for the natural world, and create awareness of the fragile underwater world, creative communities, pioneering research, ancient crafts and traditions, and the conscious collaboration of people and planet.

Its Marine Discovery Centre is an interactive research, conservation and education facility which aims to protect the creatures of Maldives' only UNESCO World Biosphere Reserve and houses The Manta Trust. The resort shines a sustainable spotlight on traditional arts and crafts, employs local Bodu beru (big drum) bands to promote cultural dance, supports lacquerware artisans and a co-operative that produces the coral frames used in its Reefscapers coral propagation project. Their community support extends to sponsoring an elementary teacher's salary, a Football Challenge to strengthen community bonds at Baa's 13 islands, a Parley for the Oceans project to collect plastic waste to be recycled into sportswear, and their Four Seasons Hospitality Apprenticeship which has graduated more than 640 Maldivian students. The resort's solar roof installations saves around 300,000 litres of diesel annually, a carbon reduction of 650-800 tons.

Das Biosphärenreservat Baa Atoll umfasst 75 Inseln auf den Malediven und birgt eine der größten Gruppen von Korallenriffen im Indischen Ozean. Landaa Giraavaru ist eine geschützte, 44 Hektar große Inselwildnis im Baa-Atoll mit dem luxuriösen Four Seasons Resort, das von weißen Sandstränden und türkisfarbenen Lagune umgeben ist. Ein passionierter Geschäftsführer – Armando Kraenzlin – und ein hochmotiviertes Team fühlen sich ermutigt, Naturverbundenheit und Wertschätzung der natürlichen Umgebung zu pflegen und ein Bewusstsein für die fragile Unterwasserwelt, kreative Gemeinschaften, wegweisende Forschung, traditionelles Kunsthandwerk sowie die bewusste Zusammenarbeit von Mensch und Planet zu schaffen.

Das Marine Discovery Center ist eine interaktive Forschungs-, Naturschutz- und Bildungseinrichtung, die darauf abzielt, die Lebewesen des einzigen UNESCO-Weltbiosphärenreservats der Malediven zu schützen. Das Forschungszentrum beherbergt u. a. den Manta Trust zum Schutz von Mantarochen. Das Resort rückt die Nachhaltigkeit des traditionellen Kunsthandwerks in den Fokus, beschäftigt lokale Bodu Beru-Trommlergruppen zur Förderung des kulturellen Tanzes, unterstützt das Kunsthandwerk der Lackkunst und eine Kooperative zur Herstellung von Korallenrahmen für das Korallenvermehrungsprojekt Reefscapers. Ihr kommunaler Beitrag erstreckt sich auf das Sponsoring eines Grundschullehrergehalts, einer Football-Challenge zur Stärkung der Gemeinschaftsbande auf den 13 Baa-Inseln, eines Parley for the Oceans-Projekt zum Sammeln von Plastikmüll, der zu Sportkleidung recycelt wird, und auf das Four Seasons-Hotelfachlehre mit bisher über 640 maledivischen Absolventen. Die Solardachanlagen des Resorts bringen eine Ersparnis von jährlich rund 300.000 Litern Diesel, was einem CO_2-Äquivalent von 650-800 Tonnen entspricht.

Guests can help to rehabilitate sea turtles at the Marine Discovery Centre, support reef restoration projects with unique coral frame techniques, join the Maldives' only full-time manta ray research project and snorkel with mass gatherings of manta rays.

Gäste können im Marine Discovery Centre bei der Ansiedlung von Meeresschildkröten helfen oder die Wiederherstellung natürlicher Riffe mit einzigartigen Korallen unterstützen, außerdem können sie dem einzigen Vollzeit-Forschungsprojekt der Malediven über Manta-Rochen beiwohnen und mit den majestätischen Tieren schnorcheln.

THE DATAI, MALAYSIA

Retreat To Ancient Nature

Overlooking the Andaman Sea, The Datai is nestled in Lankawi island's glorious wilderness, a UNESCO geopark created by forces of nature half a billion years ago off the coast of west Malaysia. Guests can experience profound sensory wellbeing with nature's calming sounds while wandering, meditating and forest bathing, and with Ramuan culture's age-old rituals and rainforest botanical blends to beautify and restore. They can discover the sea, mangroves and ancient rainforest with resident naturalists and marine biologists, learn about Malay, Thai and Indian ingredients and traditional cooking from resident chefs, harvest honey from the hive, and learn permaculture and upcycle in The Lab. And most life-changing, they can consciously give back by taking part and supporting The Datai Pledge, a trust launched in 2019 to improve the wellbeing of Lankawi's environment, wildlife, and local community.

The Datai's passionate GM - Arnaud Girodon - leads an inspired team and serves as Board Trustee to The Datai Pledge which funds the research, conservation and sustainability efforts of NGOs and social enterprise partners. It has four pillars: PURE focuses on sustainable business operations and regenerates the environment and community. FISH aims to conserve coral reefs and marine life and promotes sustainable fishing. WILDLIFE focuses on conserving wildlife and regenerating the rainforests. YOUTH aims to nurture appreciation of nature through education. Together, they are attaining their earnest goals for carbon reduction, zero waste to landfill targets, supporting marginalised indigenous communities, and forging resilience and hope for a better future.

Mit Blick auf die Andamanensee liegt das Datai Bay Resort in der herrlichen Wildnis der Insel Lankawi, einem UNESCO-Geopark, der vor einer halben Jahrmilliarde vor der Küste Westmalaysias von Naturgewalten erschaffen wurde. Die Gäste können, begleitet von beruhigenden Naturgeräuschen beim Wandern, Meditieren und Waldbaden, ein tiefes sinnliches Wohlbefinden erleben oder auch Schönheits- und Erholungsrituale der Ramuan-Spakultur mit botanischen Mischungen des Regenwaldes zelebrieren. Sie können mit ortsansässigen Natur- und Meereskundlern das Meer, Mangroven und den alten Regenwald entdecken und von Gastköchen etwas über malaiische, thailändische und indische Zutaten und Traditionsküche lernen, Honig aus dem Bienenstock ernten und in der Experimentierstätte „The Lab" Permakultur und Upcycling erlernen. 2019 wurde zum Wohl der Ortsgemeinschaft The Datai Pledge ins Leben gerufen. Durch aktive Teilnahme können die Gäste dem Land bewusst etwas zurückgeben und durch Unterstützung dieser Initiative einen wirklich lebensverändernden Beitrag leisten.

Der passionierte Geschäftsführer Arnaud Girodon leitet ein begeistertes Team und fungiert als Gremien-Mitglied für die Stiftung zur Finanzierung von Forschungs-, Naturschutz- und Nachhaltigkeitsbestrebungen von NGOs und Sozialpartnern. Ihr Engagement beruht auf vier Säulen: PURE konzentriert sich auf zukunftsfähigen Geschäftsbetrieb und findet Strategien zur Erneuerung der Umwelt und der Ortsgemeinde. FISH zielt darauf ab, Korallenriffe und Meereslebewesen zu erhalten und eine nachhaltige Fischerei zu fördern. WILDLIFE konzentriert sich auf den Artenschutz und die Regenerierung der Regenwälder. YOUTH möchte durch Bildung die Wertschätzung der Natur fördern. Im Zusammenwirken erreichen sie ihre ehrlichen Ziele wie CO_2-Reduktion, Null-Abfall-Produktion, Unterstützung marginalisierter indigener Gemeinschaften und Stärkung der Resilienz, um Hoffnung auf eine bessere Zukunft zu schmieden.

Guests can walk down to the beach through a verdant rainforest with hornbills, gibbons, and tropical flora and fauna to enjoy yoga and watersports or a romantic dinner at sunset.

Page 56-57: The hillside resort with rooms, restaurants and pools embraces the rainforest.

Die Gäste können durch einen grünen Regenwald mit Nashornvögeln, Gibbons und tropischer Flora und Fauna zum Strand hinunterwandern, und dort Yoga und Wassersport betreiben oder ein romantisches Abendessen bei Sonnenuntergang genießen.

Seite 56-57: Das am Hang gelegene Resort mit Zimmern, Restaurants und Pools liegt inmitten des Regenwaldes.

The open-air Nature Centre offers a library of Langkawi and Malaysia's natural world. Guests can view nature up close from suspended bridges between trees, learn Malay martial art and yoga.

Page 62-63: Guests can step from their bed to the swimming pool. Spa villa with lotus flowers in bloom.

Das Nature Centre unter freiem Himmel bietet eine natürliche Bibliothek der Umwelt Langkawis und Malaysias. Die Gäste können die Natur aus nächster Nähe von Hängebrücken betrachten sowie malaiische Kampfkunst und Yoga erlernen.

Seite 60-61: Die Gäste können von ihrem Bett aus in den Swimmingpool steigen und in der Spa-Villa blühende Lotosblumen bewundern.

BAWAH RESERVE, INDONESIA

Above, Below And Beyond

At the bottom of Indonesia's Anambas Archipelago, the islands of Bawah flourish with lush verdant nature, rare flora and fauna species, ancient trees, mangrove and coral reef biodiversity hotspots and clear crystal waters. A vision to protect, enhance and sustain inspired its owner Tim Hartnoll and a creative team to consciously build Bawah Reserve with local hands and materials, power by solar and ensure minimal impact to six pristine islands, 13 white-sand beaches and three turquoise lagoons.

Opened in late 2017, Tim and a vibrantly conscious COO Paul Robinson mentor a willing local team and suppliers to be circular and help sustain their natural heritage and ensure that money goes into local pockets. Its inspiring ethos works on three levels: ABOVE focuses on what is built and grown and looks after the forest, flora and fauna. BELOW focuses on the ocean, the rain and water to drink. BEYOND is about people and their impact on the 'above' and 'below'.

The secluded Bawah Reserve has defined luxury to be authentic, caring, grounded, spacious and comfortable with a sense of place, where guests can feel revitalized, embrace conservation learning and immerse in nature. Guests can dive with biologists, join a permaculture tour of organic gardens and Indonesian cuisine cookery class, and enjoy water activities in a protected reef and blue lagoon. Guest stays, purchases and donations give back generously to the Anambas Foundation, which safeguards biodiversity through a marine and land-based conservation program, and lift the welfare and resilience of Anambas island communities.

Am südlichsten Ende des indonesischen Anambas-Archipels gedeihen die Bawah-Inseln mit üppig grüner Natur, seltener Vielfalt von Flora und Fauna, uralten Bäumen sowie Hotspots der Biodiversität mit Mangroven, Korallenriffen und kristallklarem Gewässern. Eine Vision des Schützens, Aufwertens und Förderns inspirierte seinen Eigentümer Tim Hartnoll und ein kreatives Team, das Bawah Reserve bewusst mit Menschen und Materialien lokaler Herkunft zu bauen und – zur bestmöglichen Schonung von sechs unberührten Inseln, 13 weißen Sandstränden und drei türkisfarbenen Lagunen – mit Sonnenenergie zu betreiben.

Seit Eröffnung im Jahr 2017 betreuen Tim und ein souverän agierender Geschäftsführer – Paul Robinson – ein engagiertes Team aus Locals und lokalen Anbietern, um zirkulär zu arbeiten, zum Erhalt ihres Naturerbes beizutragen und sicherzustellen, dass Geld in die lokalen Taschen fließt. Der inspirierende Resort-Slogan wirkt auf drei Ebenen: ABOVE setzt auf das Gebaute und Gewachsene und kümmert sich um Wald, Flora und Fauna. BELOW widmet sich schwerpunktmäßig dem Meer, dem Regen und dem Trinkwasser. BEYOND handelt von Menschen und ihren Einfluss auf das „Oben" und „Unten".

Das Hideaway-Resort definiert Luxus als authentisch, mitmenschlich, bodenständig, weitläufig und komfortabel mit der belebenden Aura eines Orts, wo die Gäste in die Natur eintauchen und etwas über Arten- und Naturschutz lernen können, sei es auf wissenschaftlich geleiteten Unterwassersafaris, im Rahmen geführter Touren durch Permakulturgärten, durch Teilnahme an einem Kochkurs für indonesische Küche oder bei Wasseraktivitäten in einem geschützten Riff und in einer blauen Lagune. Über Gastaufenthalte, Ankäufe und Schenkungen fließen der Anambas Foundation reichlich Gelder zu. Mithilfe eines Meeres- und Landschutzprogramms schützt die Stiftung die Biodiversität und stärkt das Wohl und die Widerstandsfähigkeit der Inselkommunen.

Guests can enjoy other islands for a beach picnic and walk up to mountain cliffs to view incredible vistas and the whole Atoll.

Page 66: Guests arrive in an open-air jetty and walk across a boardwalk to Bawah Reserve.

Page 72-73: Designer Sim Boon Yang of Eco-ID Architect realized the owner's vision.

Die Gäste können auf anderen Inseln ein Strandpicknick machen und zu den Bergklippen hinaufwandern, um unglaubliche Ausblicke und das gesamte Atoll zu genießen.

Seite 66: Die Gäste kommen an einem Steg an und erreichen über eine Holzpromenade das Bawah-Reserve.

Seite 72-73: Der Designer Sim Boon Yang von Eco-ID Architect setzte die Vision des Eigentümers um.

The Aura Wellness Centre and Spa lounge offers rejuvenation treatments. A seaplane pilot takes guests to Bawa Reserve and sets the mood for barefoot travel. Guests can enjoy dinner on the beach by candlelight.

Page 74-75: Tree Tops Restaurant on a cliff with a view of the ocean.

Das Aura Wellness Centre und die Spa-Lounge bieten Verjüngungskuren an. Ein Wasserflugzeugpilot bringt die Gäste zum Bawa-Reserve und stimmt sie auf den Barfußurlaub ein. Das Abendessen können die Gäste bei Kerzenlicht am Strand genießen.

Seite 74-75: Das Tree Tops Restaurant sitzt auf einer Klippe mit Blick auf den Ozean.

BAMBU INDAH, BALI, INDONESIA

A Jungle Wonderland

Ubud is a lively town with a chilled and cultural vibe in the Indonesian island of Bali. It is a place to explore culture and history, discover the work of local artists and sustainably creative artisans, visit ancient temples and healing centers, work as a digital nomad, and walk at a slow pace surrounded by emerald-green rice terraces and steep ravines.

Bambu Indah (Balinese for 'beautiful bamboo') is a sustainably minded jungle retreat, lovingly curated by conscious designers and owners – John and Cynthia Hardy – in the lush and quaint village of Baung. Built from local materials, there are antique Javanese bridal houses, delightfully designed open bamboo structures and houses nestled in trees and by the river, and jungle tents on floating platforms at a cliff overlook the valley.

Guests are welcomed with a water purification ritual and offered modern luxury service and comfort (including air-conditioning!) in a smoke-free environment. The waste is recycled and the drinking water is carefully filtered. Organic bath and spa products are available for guests. Delicious local cuisine is nourishing, with organic produce regeneratively grown by gardener staff who are paid extra for the yield they harvest. Guests can join an early morning rice padi walk and pick up trash. The ultimate holiday feeling goes hand in hand with a Balinese wellness package; this includes traditional massage and yoga classes under local direction and lazy hours in natural spring plunge pools made of lava stone instead of concrete, and last but not least, moon bathe in a copper tub. Eco-loving guests wanting to explore should visit the Green Village, the Green School, the Bamboo Pure Factory and the Sunday Farmers Markets for local food and spices, handmade jewelry and plant-dyed Indonesian textiles by local artisans.

Ubud ist eine lebhafte Stadt mit lässiger, kulturdurchdrungener Atmosphäre auf der indonesischen Insel Bali. Es ist ein Ort, um Kultur und Geschichte zu erkunden, die Arbeit indonesischer Künstler und nachhaltig schaffender Kunsthandwerker zu entdecken, alte Tempel und Heilzentren zu besuchen, als Digitalnomade zu arbeiten und zu entschleunigen, umgeben von smaragdgrünen Reisterrassen und tiefen Schluchten.

Bambu Indah (balinesisch für „schöner Bambus") ist ein nachhaltig gesinntes Dschungel-Retreat, das von selbstbewussten Designern und Eigentümern – John und Cynthia Hardy – in der tropisch üppigen Idylle des Dorfes Baung umhegt und gepflegt wird. Mit lokalen Materialien erbaut, liegen die antiken javanischen Brauthäuser, die herrlich offen gestalteten Bambushäuser und Bungalows eingebettet in das Dickicht des Waldes oder vom Fluss umschlungen. An einer Klippe auf Holzdecks schwebende Bubble-Zelte überblicken das Tal.

Die Gäste werden mit einer rituellen Waschung begrüßt und mit modernen Luxus und Komfort (einschließlich Klimaanlage!) in einer rauchfreien Umgebung verwöhnt. Die Abfälle werden recycelt, das Trinkwasser wird sorgfältig gefiltert. Für die Gäste stehen Spa-Produkte in Bioqualität bereit. Die lokale Küche schmeckt nicht nur köstlich, sondern enthält auch Bio-Zutaten aus regenerativer Permakultur, wie sie vor Ort praktiziert wird. Alle Gärtner werden für das Ernten extra bezahlt. Die Gäste können am frühen Morgen an einem Ramadama-Spaziergang durch die Reisfelder teilnehmen. Das ultimative Urlaubsfeeling geht mit einem balinesischen Wellnesspaket einher; dazu gehören traditionelle Massage- und Yoga-Kurse unter einheimischer Leitung, faule Stunden in natürlichen Lavabecken (statt Betonbassins) und – last but not least – ein Mondbad in einer Kupferwanne. Umweltfreundliche Gäste mit Lust auf Erkundungstouren in die nähere Umgebung sollten das Grüne Dorf, die Grüne Schule, die Reiner-Bambus-Fabrik und die sonntäglichen Bauernmärkte besuchen; dort kann man lokale Lebensmittel und Gewürze, Schmuck und pflanzengefärbte Textilien von indonesischen Kunsthandwerkern erstehen.

Bambu Indah offers creative surprises. Copper villa suite with copper bathtub and over-water hanging lounge seats.

Page 80-81: The daily Balinese offering ritual. Guests can climb spiral staircase to explore cliffs and cross bamboo bridges over a gorge.

Bambu Indah bietet kreative Überraschungen: Kupfervilla-Suite mit passender Kupferbadewanne und über dem Wasser hängenden Lounge-Sitzen.

Seite 80-81: Ein balinesisches Opferritual wird täglich durchgeführt. Gäste können über Wendeltreppen die Klippen erklimmen und Bambusbrücken über eine Schlucht überqueren.

The inspiring John and Cynthia Hardy and daughter Elora are behind the retreat's wonderland magic and creativity. Elora founded the company IBUKU and designed the oyster and mushroom shaped structures at Bamboo Indah and a community of unique bamboo homes in Bali.

Die inspirierenden John und Cynthia Hardy und ihre Tochter Elora stehen hinter dem Zauber und der Kreativität dieses wundervollen Rückzugortes. Elora gründete das Unternehmen IBUKU und entwarf die austern- und pilzförmigen Strukturen von Bamboo Indah sowie eine Ansammlung einzigartiger Bambushäuser auf Bali.

THE LEGIAN SEMINYAK, BALI, INDONESIA

Eat, Pray And Love Better

Indonesia is a country in South East Asia with over 17,000 islands, two of which – Bali and Lombok – have enchanted people with different walks of life: the culturally curious, digital nomads, earth loving hippies, expat residents, love birds and honeymooners, paradise explorers, partying backpackers, soul surfers, wellness seekers, and more.

Bali is in the Lesser Sunda Islands with a spiritual culture immersed in Hinduism. Its massive tourism sphere can pack fascinating vacation adventures in ancient temples, jungle parks, volcanic landscapes, sandy beaches, and wild nightclubs. The millions of tourists each year have a positive economic impact on Bali, but its density, uncontrolled development and poor waste management have cost the island its pristine state and traditional authenticity and harmed its ecosystem. Separated by a narrow strait, the island of Lombok is in West Nusa Tenggara Province and seeks to promote its Islamic heritage and Muslim-friendly destination. It has a laid-back vibe with less tourism, idyllic beaches and authentic traditional communities.

In Bali, the islanders are warm and friendly, and they maintain a spiritual relationship with the natural world which powers their beliefs and essence as a human being, their culture and heritage. The source of their creativity is handicrafts, which produce all kinds of beautiful artifacts and pieces of art. They have proudly adapted their culture to fit with changing times and welcome travellers, but tourism's negative impacts are clearly harming the environment, wildlife and human health, and there is increasing pollution, especially plastic waste. Forces with a broad coalition of islanders are driving change and a few hotels are also leading the way.

The Legian Seminyak in Bali is a private and peaceful resort surrounded by lush tropical landscaped gardens on the finest stretch of Seminyak Beach. The newly opened The Legian Sire, on the other hand, is situated on Lombok's most pristine beach with stunning views of Gili Islands. Chief Operating Officer Hans Joerg Meier

Indonesien ist ein Land in Südostasien mit über 17.000 Inseln. Zwei davon – Bali und Lombok – ziehen verschiedenste Menschen in ihren Bann: Kulturinteressierte, Digitalnomaden, erdverliebte Hippies, Auswanderer, Turteltäubchen und Hochzeitsreisende, Paradiesforscher, Party-Backpacker, Soul Surfer, Wellness-Suchende und viele andere.

Bali liegt auf den Kleinen Sunda-Inseln, deren Kultur tief im Hinduismus verwurzelt ist. Seine stark ausgeprägte Tourismuswelt wartet mit faszinierenden Urlaubserlebnissen in alten Tempeln, Dschungelparks, Vulkanlandschaften, Sandstränden und ausschweifenden Partys in Nachtclubs auf. Die Millionen Gäste jedes Jahr haben einen positiven wirtschaftlichen Einfluss auf Bali, aber ihre Dichte, unkontrollierte Entwicklung und schlechtes Abfallmanagement haben der Insel ihre Ursprünglichkeit und Authentizität gekostet und das Ökosystem geschädigt. Die durch eine schmale Meerenge getrennte Insel Lombok liegt in der Provinz West Nusa Tenggara und ist als muslimophile Destination sehr auf ihr islamisches Erbe bedacht. Dort herrscht eine entspannte Atmosphäre mit weniger Tourismus, idyllischen Stränden und authentischen traditionellen Ortsgemeinden.

Die Inselbewohner auf Bali sind warmherzig und freundlich. Sie hegen eine spirituelle Beziehung zur Natur, was ihren Glauben und ihr menschliches Wesen, ihre Kultur und ihr Erbe antreibt. Quelle ihrer Kreativität ist das Kunsthandwerk, dass allerlei schöne Artefakte und Kunstwerke hervorbringt. Sie haben ihre Kultur stolz an die sich verändernden Zeiten angepasst und heißen Reisende willkommen, hingegen erweist sich der Tourismus – insbesondere die Umweltverschmutzung durch Plastikmüll – als sichtbar belastend für Mensch, Umwelt und Wildnis. Es gibt seitens der Insulaner starke Triebkräfte der Transformation und auch einige Hotels sind darin wegweisend.

Das Legian Seminyak auf Bali ist ein beschauliches Resort mit Privatsphäre, umgeben von üppigen tropischen Landschaftsgärten

The Legian Bali is on Seminyak Beach, a hip and swinging place favored by great waves. The hotel décor and gardens celebrate the local Balinese culture, tradition and geography, the iconic trademark of designer Jaya Ibrahim. Every suite has spectacular ocean views.

Das Legian Bali liegt am Strand von Seminyak, einem hippen und lebendigen Ort, der von großen Wellen umwogt wird. Das Hoteldekor und die Gärten zelebrieren die lokale balinesische Kultur, Tradition und Geografie, unterstrichen durch die ikonische Gestaltung des Designers Jaya Ibrahim. Jede Suite bietet einen spektakulären Blick auf das Meer.

The resort offers extraordinary settings for celebrations and weddings. The spa is holistic and nurturing and draws on local culture and indigenous healing traditions. A nutritionist curates the menus and recipes using locally and regionally sourced organic ingredients.

Das Resort bietet einen außergewöhnlichen Rahmen für Feiern und Hochzeiten. Das Spa ist ganzheitlich organisiert und stützt sich auf die lokale Kultur und indigene Heiltraditionen. Ein Ernährungswissenschaftler stellt die Menüs und Rezepte aus lokalen und regionalen Bio-Zutaten zusammen.

THE LEGIAN SIRE, LOMBOK, INDONESIA

leads an inspired team to be rigorous on sustainability. They are passionate about protecting the environment and supporting local communities. To reduce waste, packaging (glass, paper, plastic) is separated and recycled, a water filtering and bottling plant eliminate single-use plastic, and wastewater is recycled and used for watering the gardens. Locally-made organic amenities are provided in refillable ceramic bottles. Lighting is LED to conserve energy. Conscious about conservation, they clean their beaches daily, use biodegradable cleaning products and 100% natural mosquito repellent, and turtle eggs that are laid on its beachfront are protected, harvested, shielded until they hatch in a Turtle Nursery, then released with staff and guests.

They support their community by hiring local staff and guides, buy locally and organically when available, and showcase local artists, Indonesian artefacts and celebrate traditional culture. In 2008, inspiring women managers founded Team 8, an initiative dedicated to assist local schools, a therapy centre for children with cerebral palsy, and a local elderly home with vital equipment and support. With their deep connection to the communities, environment and nature, coupled with the culture and heritage of the destination, both resorts intend to create meaningful authentic life experiences and memories to treasure.

am schönsten Strandabschnitt des Seminyak Beach. Das neu eröffnete Legian Sire hingegen liegt am unberührtesten Strand von Lombok mit atemberaubendem Blick auf die Gili-Inseln. Hans Jörg Meier leitet ein inspiriertes Team, das konsequent auf Nachhaltigkeit setzt. Legian setzt sich leidenschaftlich dafür ein, die Umwelt zu schützen und Ortsgemeinden zu unterstützen. Um Abfall zu reduzieren, werden Verpackungen (Glas, Papier, Kunststoff) getrennt und recycelt, in einer Wasserfilter- und Abfüllanlage werden Einwegkunststoffe eliminiert, Gärten werden mit Grauwasser bewässert. Lokal hergestellte Bio-Pflegeprodukte gibt es in nachfüllbaren Keramikflaschen. Mit LED-Beleuchtung wird Strom gespart. Im Einklang mit dem Artenschutzgedanken werden die Hotelstrände täglich gesäubert und biologisch abbaubare Reinigungsprodukte sowie 100% natürliche Mückenschutzmittel verwendet. Am Strand abgelegte Schildkröteneier werden zum Ausbrüten in eine Aufzuchtstation verbracht. Personal und Gäste helfen gemeinsam beim Auswildern der Küken nach dem Schlüpfen.

Die Ortsgemeinde wird durch Einstellung von Locals und indonesischen Gästeführern unterstützt. Sofern genügend Angebot vorhanden ist, wird lokal und biologisch eingekauft. Im Fokus stehen einheimische Künstler, indonesische Artefakte und traditionelle Kultur. 2008 gründeten Managerinnen mit großem Inspirationsgeist Team 8, eine Hilfsinitiative für lokale Schulen, ein Therapiezentrum für Kinder mit Zerebralparese und ein Seniorenheim mit lebenswichtiger Ausstattung und Betreuungsdienstleistungen. In ihrer tiefen Verbundenheit mit den Inselkommunen, der Umwelt und der Natur, gepaart mit der Kultur und dem Erbe der Destination, wollen beide Resorts bedeutungsvolle authentische Lebenserfahrungen und wertvolle Erinnerungen schaffen.

The calm and timeless interior celebrates local culture and craftsmanship. Two-tiered swimming pool and suites have an ocean-facing private terraces.

Page 98–101: Located on Sire Beach, the all-suite and villa resort has views towards Gili islands and Bali's Mount Agung.

Die ruhige und zeitlose Einrichtung zelebriert die lokale Kultur und Handwerkskunst. Der Swimmingpool ist zweistufig und die Suiten haben eine private Terrasse mit Meerblick.

Seite 98-101: Das am Sire Beach gelegene Resort besteht nur aus Suiten und Villen mit Blick auf die Gili-Inseln und den Mount Agung auf Bali.

SONG SAA, CAMBODIA

The Ethical Sweethearts

The two islets known as Song Saa (Khmer for 'the sweethearts') are a 35-minute boat ride from Sihanoukville's port in Cambodia, connected by a wooden footbridge over a gentle sea and marine reserve. This is the secluded Song Saa Private Island, a tranquil luxury retreat with a delightful immaterial dimension, where guests are nourished and restored by nature, are reconnected with simple wonders and themselves. Enchanted by Khmer culture and heritage, they feel deeply fulfilled here while contributing to economic prosperity.

A Discovery Center provides conservation knowledge and time spent with local guides to explore mangrove forests, to view how coral is grown, to nurture and plant tree seedlings is a galvanizing and transformative experience. The Song Saa Foundation action three vibrant projects that put People and Planet first. People projects focus on education programs, medical missions, and organic farming support. Land projects protect resources and scale conservation by constructing water catchments, distributing water filters, managing solid waste, and actioning tree planting to restore ecosystems. Water projects aim to preserve marine life and protect ocean habitats by supporting fisheries, a coral nursery, a turtle conservation, planting thousands of mangroves, and tracking reef diversity and sea grass growth. The resort hosts are its inspiring custodians, committed to sustainability and aim to be climate positive before 2030. A passionate Founder and CEO Melita Koulmandas, an inspired team and habitants are bonded by purpose and the holistic impact of their brilliant work in conservation and regeneration enhance local livelihoods, build resilience, harness joy, and sustain lives.

Die zwei Inselchen namens Song Saa ("Khmer für "Schätzchen") sind eine 35-minütige Bootsfahrt vom Hafen von Sikahnoukville in Kambodscha entfernt und durch eine hölzerne Fußgängerbrücke über ein sanftes Meeresschutzgebiet verbunden. Dort befindet sich die abgeschiedene Privatinsel Song Saa, ein ruhiges Luxus-Retreat mit einer reizvollen geistigen Dimension, wo Gäste in und mit der Natur neue Lebenskraft tanken und mit einfachen Wundern und sich selbst wieder verbunden werden. Bezaubert von der Kultur und dem Erbe der Khmer, fühlen sie sich hier zutiefst erfüllt und tragen gleichzeitig zur wirtschaftlichen Prosperität bei.

In einem Forschungszentrum Wissen zu teilen und auf Erkundungstouren in den Mangrovenwäldern, in der Korrallenzucht und in der Baumschule seine Zeit mit lokalen Guides zu verbringen, ist ein aufregendes und transformatives Erlebnis. Die Song Saa Foundation setzt drei lebendige Projekte um, bei denen Mensch und Planet an erster Stelle stehen. People-Projekte befassen sich schwerpunktmäßig mit Bildungsprogrammen, medizinischer Versorgung und der Förderung des ökologischen Landbaus. Land- und Bodenprojekte schützen Ressourcen und dimensionieren den Naturschutz durch Wasserspeicher in Einzugsgebieten, Verteilung von Wasserfiltern, Management von Feststoffabfall und Baumpflanzungen zur Sanierung von Ökosystemen. Wasserprojekte wollen die Unterwasserwelt erhalten und Meereshabitate schützen, indem sie die Fischerei, eine Korallengärtnerei, Schildkrötenschutz, Mangrovenaufforstung im großen Stil sowie Riffvielfalt und Seegraswachstum nachverfolgen. Die Gastgeber verstehen sich als inspirierende Nachhaltigkeitswächter, die noch vor 2030 klimapositiv werden wollen. Die passionierte Gründerin und Geschäftsführerin Melita Koulmandas, ein begeistertes Team und die Einwohner schaffen mit ihrer exzellenten, sinnstiftenden Arbeit einen ganzheitlichen Impact zur Stärkung lokaler Lebensgrundlagen, zum Aufbau von Resilienz und zum Erhalt von Leben und Lebensfreude.

An intimate escape where guests can tune into simple luxuries - a pristine beach, spacious wooden villas, spa sanctuaries and a preserved coral reef. Jungle villas with a view offer open-plan living spaces with a private pool.

Page 106-107: A wooden boardwalk connect the islands and villas.

Ein Zufluchtsort, an dem sich die Gäste auf einfachen Luxus einstellen können - einen unberührten Strand, geräumige Holzvillen, Spa-Zentren und ein Korallenriff. Die Dschungelvillen mit besonderer Aussicht bieten offene Wohnbereiche mit einem privaten Pool.

Seite 106-107: Eine Holzpromenade verbindet die Inseln und Villen.

Song Saa offers surprising experiences and adventures. Enjoy a local snack and floating lotuses. Have a romantic dinner on the pool with a view and bare feet touching cool water, dive beneath the waves, hike through the hills and retreat for detox, well-being and relaxation.

Song Saa bietet überraschende Erlebnisse und Abenteuer. Genehmigen Sie sich einen lokalen Snack und bewundern Sie schwimmende Lotusblumen. Genießen Sie ein romantisches Abendessen am Pool mit Aussicht – barfuß im kühlenden Wasser –, tauchen Sie in die Wellen, wandern Sie durch die Hügel und ziehen Sie sich zum Entgiften, Wohlfühlen und Entspannen zurück.

NAM HAI FOUR SEASONS, VIETNAM

Living In The Moment

The Four Seasons Resort The Nam Hai stretches for a half mile on Ha My beach in Vietnam's central coast, a tranquil and authentic escape with lush tropical nature, delightful birds and frogs, warm Vietnamese hospitality, and a deep connection to this culturally rich region. Guests can experience traditional wellness remedies and cooking with ingredients from onsite organic gardens, creative local arts and crafts classes, and a weekly candle lighting ritual to pray to ancestors for peace, health, happiness, and great fortune. There are also three fascinating UNESCO sites (the imperial city of Hue, the sanctuary of My Son and the ancient city of Hoi An) to be discovered. And epicures can join a culinary guided tour by Vespa to savour local eatery specialties.

Wellbeing spa experiences are based on the mindfullness philosophy of Vietnamese Buddhist monk Thich Nhat Hanh, and focus on the present to gain insight, find joy and happiness and gently restore. Each evening, healing vibrations from crystal singing bowls fill the spa, and guests are invited to write their thoughts on paper, place it in a paper lantern to gracefully float in a pond, and bid 'goodnight' to Mother Earth.

A conscious GM - Blaise Montandon - mentored a willing team to action sustainability practices to consume and waste less, to not compromise, and to be mindful in their work and in their private lives. They initiated a water bottling plant project to stop the staggering single-use plastic bottle waste, actioned a circular approach to food waste, and support the local community by hiring 95% locally, purchasing locally, providing internship experiences, and training to hone actionable knowledge and life skills for a better life.

Das Four Seasons Resort Nam Hai erstreckt sich über einen Kilometer am Strand von Ha My an der zentralen Küste Vietnams, einem ruhigen und authentischen Zufluchtsort mit üppiger tropischer Natur, bezaubernden Vögeln und Fröschen, herzlicher vietnamesischer Gastfreundschaft und einer tiefen Verbundenheit mit dieser kulturell reichen Region. Die Gäste können traditionelle Wellness-Heilmittel und Kochzutaten aus den lokalen Biogärten kennenlernen, an Kunsthandwerkskursen teilnehmen und bei einem wöchentlichen Kerzenanzündungsritual die Ahnen um Frieden, Gesundheit, Glück und großes Vermögen anrufen. Zudem wollen drei faszinierende UNESCO-Stätten (die Kaiserstadt Hue, das Heiligtum von My Son und die antike Stadt Hoi An) entdeckt werden. Genießer können im Rahmen einer kulinarischen Vespa-Tour Spezialitäten verkosten.

Die dort erlebbare Wellnesskultur basiert auf der Achtsamkeitsphilosophie des vietnamesischen, buddhistischen Mönchs Thich Nhat Hanh und ist gegenwartszentriert, um Einsichten zu gewinnen, Freude und Glück zu finden und sich auf sanfte Art zu regenerieren. Jeden Abend ist das Spa mit heilsamen Schwingungen von Kristallklangschalen erfüllt, und die Gäste werden aufgefordert, ihre Gedanken auf Wunschzettel zu schreiben, um sie dann – als Gute-Nacht-Gruß an Mutter Erde – in Papierlaternen, die sie dann auf einem Teich dahingleiten lassen.

Der selbstbewusste Geschäftsführer Blaise Montandon hat ein aufgeschlossenes Team angeleitet, Nachhaltigkeit praktisch zu leben, weniger zu konsumieren und weniger wegzuwerfen, konsequent zu sein und in ihrer Arbeit wie auch im Privatleben achtsam zu sein. Auf ihre Initiative hin wurde eine Wasserabfüllanlage gebaut, um das enorme Müllaufkommen durch Einweg-Plastikflaschen zu stoppen. Sie ergriffen eine zirkuläre Strategie gegen Lebensmittelverschwendung und die Ortsgemeinde erfährt Unterstützung, indem zu 95% Locals eingestellt werden. Es wird lokal eingekauft, und es gibt Praktika und Schulungen, um valides Wissen zu perfektionieren und Lebenskompetenzen zu fördern.

Ideal for those seeking a romantic escape or vacation with children, the villas feature private terraces with a view of the whitest sand beach and the South China Sea, or across the landscaped resort gardens.

Die Villen verfügen über private Terrassen mit Blick auf den weißen Sandstrand und das Südchinesische Meer oder auf die gepflegten Gärten des Resorts und sind gleichermaßen ideal für einen romantischen Urlaub oder einen Urlaub mit Kindern.

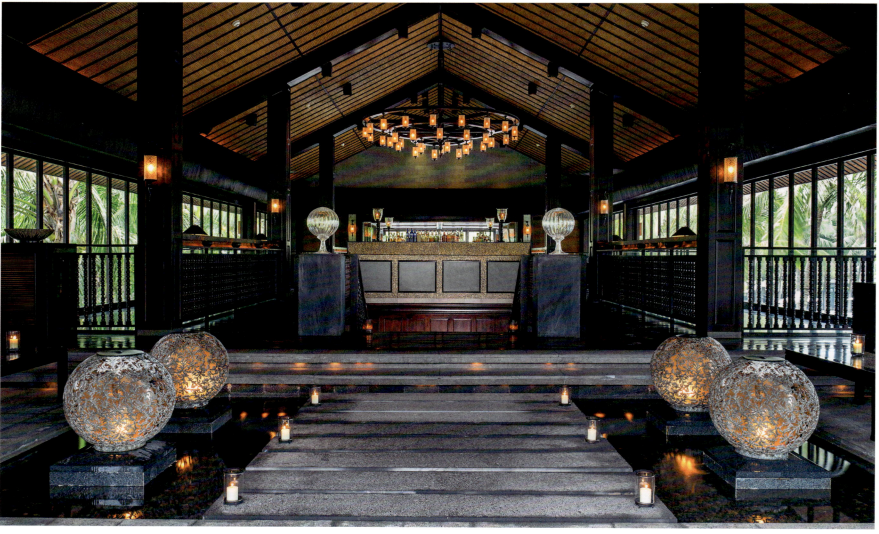

Bathing is a ritual at the spa. The Nam Hai Cooking Academy shares secrets of Vietnamese cooking.

Page 120-121: Guests can explore Hoi An's lantern-lit streets and artisan ateliers, and place lanterns with candles lit on the Thu Bon river with a wish for happiness, luck and love.

Das Baden ist ein Ritual im Spa. Die Nam Hai Cooking Academy weiht in die Geheimnisse der vietnamesischen Küche ein.

Seite 120-121: Die Gäste können die mit Laternen beleuchteten Straßen und Kunsthandwerksateliers von Hoi An erkunden sowie mit Kerzen beleuchtete Laternen auf dem Thu-Bon-Fluss aufstellen, um sich Freude, Glück und Liebe zu wünschen.

GENGHIS KHAN RETREAT, MONGOLIA

Free And Wild At Heart

In Mongolia's heartland, 200 miles west of Ulaanbaatar, Genghis Khan Retreat (GKR) overlooks the majestic valley of Orkhon National Park, where the beauty and silence of nature meets endless wilderness so vast that it links land and sky. For decades, its founder Christopher Giercke and his Mongolian wife Enkhe have returned to reconnect their children with their mother's roots, and it inspired their purpose to secure the preservation of traditional Nomadic culture and provide a livelihood and education to talented youths in the steppe.

Christopher started the Genghis Khan Polo Club in 1996, brought polo sport back to Mongolia and financed polo training for hundreds of Nomad children. He launched a unique and supremely comfortable summer adventure camp in 2015, and thus, GKR became 'the retreat place' for nature lovers and global equestrian enthusiasts to meet and mingle, ride and play polo from June to September each year. Then, they pack up and leave without a trace.

Today, the founder's valiant son - D'Artagnan - is the Polo Captain and manages GKR with the extraordinary team that helps shape the retreat, to provide guests with an intensely moving and transformative wilderness experience. GKR supports the Young Riders of the World charity and educates Nomad youths to infuse hope and bring their dreams to reality for a better life. He believes that action can cause a wind of change, that it is vital for people to transport back to a less technical lifestyle, and that seeing a simple, efficient, and versatile Nomadic lifestyle is refreshing and re-affirms that 'less is more' in a complex and globalised world. It is a testament to how humans can live with nature in a sustainable way.

In der Zentralmongolei, ca. 300 Kilometer westlich von Ulaanbaatar, überblickt das Genghis Khan Retreat (GKR) das majestätische Tal des Orchon im Nationalpark Khuisiin Naiman Nuur, wo die Schönheit und Stille der Natur auf endlose, wilde Weiten zwischen Himmel und Erde trifft. Seine Gründer – Christopher Giercke und seine mongolische Frau Enkhe – sind vor Jahrzehnten hierher zurückgekehrt, um ihre Kinder wieder mit den Wurzeln ihrer Mutter zu verbinden. Dies inspirierte sie zu ihrem Ziel, die traditionelle Nomadenkultur zu erhalten und jungen Talenten in der Steppe einen Lebensunterhalt und Bildung zu bieten.

Christopher gründete 1996 den Genghis Khan Polo Club, brachte den Reitsport zurück in die Mongolei und finanzierte das Polotraining für Hunderte von Nomadenkindern. 2015 lancierte er ein einzigartiges Sommer-Abenteuercamp mit erstklassigem Komfort, und so wurde das GKR „das" Retreat für Naturliebhaber und Pferdesportbegeisterte aus aller Welt, die sich jedes Jahr von Juni bis September zu gemeinsamen Ausritten und zum Polospiel zusammenzufinden. Danach ziehen sie wieder von dannen, ohne eine Spur zu hinterlassen.

Heute hält der beherzte Sohn des Gründers – D'Artagnan – als Polo-Captain die Zügel in der Hand und betreibt das GKR mit einem außergewöhnlichen Mitgestalterteam, um den Gästen ein tief bewegendes, transformatives Wildniserlebnis zu bieten. Das GKR unterstützt den Reitverband Young Riders of the World und bildet junge Nomaden aus, um ihnen Hoffnung auf ein besseres Lebens zu schenken. Er glaubt, dass aktives Handeln einen Wind des Wandels auslösen kann, dass es für Menschen essentiell ist, wieder mit weniger Technik zu leben, und dass es erfrischend ist zu sehen, wie gut ein einfaches, facettenreiches Nomadenleben funktioniert. Diese Lebensart bestätigt nochmals den „Weniger ist mehr"-Trend in einer komplexen, globalisierten Welt. Es ist ein Beleg dafür, wie Menschen nachhaltig mit der Natur leben können.

Genghis Khan Retreat owns around 100 riding and polo horses. The Mongolian nomad community that works at the retreat also maintains herds of sheep, goats and yaks.

Page 126-127: Guests saddle up and ride in some of the most unspoilt, rugged and breathtaking landscapes on Earth.

Das Genghis Khan Retreat besitzt rund 100 Reit- und Polopferde. Die mongolische Nomadengemeinschaft, die im Retreat arbeitet, unterhält auch Schaf-, Ziegen- und Yakherden.

Seite 126-127: Die Gäste satteln auf und reiten durch einige der unberührtesten, rauesten und atemberaubendsten Landschaften der Welt.

The retreat offers adventurous outdoor activities—archery, kayaking, rock climbing, and more.

Page 132-133: Karakorum was the administration center for the vast empire of Genghis Khan the Conqueror. Guests stay in cosy gers with crafted beds and furniture, cashmere blankets and wood-burning stoves.

Im Retreat kann man abenteuerliche Aktivitäten wie Bogenschießen, Kajakfahren, Klettern etc. nachgehen.

Seite 132-133: Karakorum war das Verwaltungszentrum des riesigen Reiches von Dschingis Khan. Heute wohnen die Gäste in gemütlichen Gers mit handgefertigten Betten und Möbeln, Kaschmirdecken und Holzöfen.

PUSHKAR CAMEL FAIR, INDIA

A Nomadic Spectacle

Pushkar is a sacred little town in the Indian state of Rajasthan, situated 14 km from Ajmer with over 14,000 residents and over 400 temples for major Hindu deities, including India's only temple for Lord Brahma - Creator of the Universe. For over 100 years, the Puskar Fair takes place during the Hindu pilgrimage season in November, a delightful spectacle of epic scale with over 200,000 visitors arriving to celebrate the pulsating Rajasthan culture, heritage, and traditions. In the winter's hazy light, priests, pilgrims, and devoted worshippers take a dip in the sacred Pushkar Lake believed to cleanse sins and surrender themselves at Brahma Temple. Nomads from the remotest deserts set up tents on sand dunes and trade thousands of camels, horses, cows, sheep, and goats.

A traditional 'shikar' camp, inspired by past desert camps of Rajasthan royal hunters, offers guests a pampered stay in luxurious tents with amenities like hot water, Indian cuisine and veranda deck chairs overlooking the fair. Tourists are enthralled by the fair's riot of colorful festivities, competitions, exhibits, music, songs, and gypsy dances performed by the bonfire at night. Decorated camels take part in beauty contests, parades and races; there are amusing bridal, longest moustache, pot races, and a tug-of-war competitions; and bazaars sell traditional hand-made arts, crafts and textiles.

Tourism, over development of facilities, water extractions for agriculture, and deforestation have negatively impacted Pushkar and the sacred lake's water quality, reducing water levels to puddles and destroying the fish population. Government actions some conservation measures and awareness programs and will need to do more.

Pushkar ist eine heilige Kleinstadt im indischen Bundesstaat Rajasthan, 14 km von Ajmer entfernt, mit über 14.000 Einwohnern und über 400 Tempeln für große hinduistische Gottheiten, darunter Indiens einziger Tempel für Lord Brahma – den Erschaffer des Universums. Seit über 100 Jahren findet während der hinduistischen Wallfahrtsaison die Puskar Fair im November statt, ein grandioses Spektakel epischen Ausmaßes mit über 200.000 Besuchern, die alle kommen, um die pulsierende Kultur, das Erbe und die Traditionen Rajasthans zu feiern. Im dunstigen Licht des Winters nehmen Priester, Pilger und Tiefgläubige ein heiliges Bad im Pushkar-See, der sie angeblich von Sünden reinwaschen soll, und übergeben dann im Brahma-Tempel ihre Seele. Nomaden aus den entlegensten Wüsten errichten Zelte auf Sanddünen und kommen mit Tausenden von Kamelen, Pferden, Kühen, Schafen und Ziegen zur Viehmesse.

Ein traditionelles „Shikar"-Camp nach dem Vorbild von früheren Wüstenlagern der königlichen Jägersmänner aus Rajasthan, bietet Gästen einen verwöhnten Aufenthalt in luxuriösen Zelten mit Annehmlichkeiten wie Warmwasser, indischer Küche und Liegestühlen auf der Veranda mit Blick auf die Messe. Touristen sind begeistert von den farbenfrohen Festen, Wettbewerben, Ausstellungen, Musik, Liedern und Zigeunertänzen, die nachts am Lagerfeuer aufgeführt werden. Geschmückte Kamele nehmen an Schönheitswettbewerben, Paraden und Rennen teil; es gibt amüsante Wettbewerbe um Bräute und längste Schnurrbärte, ein Topfrennen und ein Tauziehen; und auf Basaren werden traditionelle Artefakte, Kunsthandwerk und Textilien feilgeboten.

Tourismus, übermäßige Infrastruktur, Wasserextraktion für die Landwirtschaft und Rodungen haben sich negativ auf die Wasserqualität von Pushkar und die des heiligen Sees ausgewirkt. Der Wasserspiegel ist bis auf Pfützenniveau gesunken, die Fischpopulation zerstört. Die Regierung ergreift einige Erhaltungsmaßnahmen und Sensibilisierungsprogramme und wird noch mehr tun müssen.

The Pushkar Fair is a window into the Rajasthani culture, ancient traditions and religious beliefs. It has changed little since Mogul times, attracting cameleers and traders, Hindu faithful and global visitors. In India, the camel is the symbol of love.

Die Pushkar-Messe ist ein Einblick in die Kultur Rajasthans, in alte Traditionen und Religionen. Sie hat sich seit der Mogulzeit kaum verändert und zieht Kamelreiter und Händler, gläubige Hindus und Besucher aus aller Welt an. In Indien gilt das Kamel als Symbol der Liebe.

ADHERE AMELIA, EGYPT

The Salt Of The Good Earth

The fertile Siwa Oasis, in Egypt's Western Desert, is a nature reserve with water springs, sand dunes, highlands and wetlands, and a flourishing biodiversity. In the mid-90s, environmentalist Dr. Mounir Neamatalla´s discovery of an ancient fortress town ignited a vision and passion to help sustain the unique landscape and traditions of the oasis since 10,000 BC through sustainable development. He created the spectacular Adrère Amellal with master Berber builders, mixing rock salt and mud to naturally blend near the base of Gaafar Mountain with biblical views of infinite sand dunes, desert palms and Siwa's lakes.

It is a place where guests can experience the rarest luxury - to step back in time to an authentic and simpler world and feel sublime wellbeing in comfort and immersed in pure nature that deeply calms and transforms, detoxifies and restores, enkindles joy, and leaves the destination better. Furniture, fixtures, and carpets were handcrafted by local artisans. Nourishment is deliciously organic, grown onsite and raised in local farms. Swimming is in a natural spring and boosts immunity. Mineral labyrinth spaces have the positive power of salt to purify and heal, and are softly lit at night by beeswax candles, lanterns, torches, and thousands of stars.

As a conscious and caring partner, Dr. Neamatalla hires and purchases locally to provide a livelihood to the Berber community and initiated a women's artisan project to revive traditional embroidery. Their operations use no electricity, produce organic fertilizer and biofuel for lighting and cooking, grow organic food, gauge water use on what two natural springs can provide and aims to be Climate Positive before 2030.

Die fruchtbare Siwa-Oase in der Westwüste Ägyptens ist ein Naturschutzgebiet mit Wasserquellen, Sanddünen, Hochland und Feuchtgebieten und einer prosperierenden Biodiversität. Mitte der 1990er-Jahre entfachte die Entdeckung einer alten Festungsstadt durch den Umweltschützer Dr. Mounir Neamatalla die passionierte Vision, die einzigartige Landschaft und die Traditionen der Oase, die bis 10.000 v. Chr. zurückreichen, durch nachhaltige Entwicklung zu bewahren. Mithilfe von Berber-Baumeistern schuf er das grandiose Adrère Amellal. Für eine natürliche Landschaftssymbiose mit biblischen Ausblicken auf endlose Sanddünen, Wüstenpalmen und die Siwa-Seen ließ er am Fuße des Gaafar-Monolithen Häuser aus Salzfelsen und Lehm erbauen.

Es ist ein Ort, an dem Gäste den Luxus der seltensten Art erleben können – gleich einer Zeitreise in eine authentische, einfachere Welt, wo sie sich in herrlichem Komfort rundherum wohlfühlen. Es ist ein freudiges Eintauchen in reinste Natur, die zutiefst beruhigend und transformierend, entgiftend und regenerierend wirkt. Zudem profitiert die Destination davon: Möbel, Einrichtungsgegenstände und Teppiche wurden von lokalen Handwerkern handgefertigt. Gespeist wird auf biologisch höchstem Niveau, die Zutaten kommen aus dem regionalen Landbau. Das Schwimmen in einer Naturquelle stärkt das Immunsystem. Mineralhaltige Salzfelsen wirken reinigend und heilsam, die labyrinthartigen Wellnessräume werden nachts von Bienenwachskerzen, Laternen, Fackeln und Tausenden von Sternen sanft beleuchtet.

Als partnerschaftlich und sozial gesinnter Betreiber stellt Dr. Neamatalla Einheimische ein und kauft auch lokal ein, um für den Lebensunterhalt der Berbergemeinschaft zu sorgen. Zudem geht ein Handwerkerinnenprojekt zur Wiederbelebung traditioneller Stickerei auf seine Intiative zurück. Die EcoLodge verbraucht keinen Strom, produziert Biodünger und -brennstoff für Beleuchtung und Kochen, baut Bio-Lebensmittel an, gleicht ihren Wasserverbrauch dem Zufluss zweier natürlicher Quellen an und will bis 2030 klimapositiv sein.

A minimalist desert eco lodge offers a stay of luxurious simplicity close to the hospitable traditions of the desert Berbers. The swimming pool is shaded by a large palm grove and flows out of a natural spring. Some houses have no roofs, and the ceiling is the sky.

Eine minimalistische Öko-Lodge in der Wüste, die eine gleichermaßen einfache wie luxuriöse Unterbringung bietet, ganz in Tradition der Berberstämme. Der Swimmingpool liegt im Schatten eines großen Palmenhains und wird aus einer natürlichen Quelle gespeist. Einige Häuser haben keine Dächer und man schläft unter freiem Himmel.

Founder and host Mounir Neamatalla. Bedrooms have a comfortable bed with Egyptian cotton sheets on a platform of palm rushes, bedside tables carved from rock salt, and locally woven Berber carpet. Dinner with local organic ingredients is served in various locations each evening.

Gründer und Gastgeber Mounir Neamatalla. Die Schlafzimmer verfügen über ein bequemes Bett mit Bettwäsche aus ägyptischer Baumwolle auf einem Bettgestell aus Palmenbinsen, aus Steinsalz gehauene Nachttische und einen traditionell gewebten Berberteppich. Das Dinner mit lokalen Bio-Zutaten wird jeden Abend an einem anderen Ort serviert.

KASBAH DE TOUBKAL, MOROCCO

Moving Mountains

Kasbah du Toubkal is dramatically set in the High Atlas Mountain range of central Morocco's Toubkal National Park, a private mountain retreat in Imlil Village with a panoramic view of fertile valleys and Jbel Toubkal, North Africa's highest peak. It was a fortress ruin, sustainably restored by two inspired brothers – Mike and Chris McHugo – with a vision to develop a sustainable tourism project in a fragile mountain environment with local hands and materials in 1990. Its inspiring ethos is to enhance the lives, pride, and vitality of the local Berber community, and provide an authentic and immersive travel experience for visitors to escape, and connect with wild nature, gain insight to the Atlas Mountain environment, and sustain the Berber way of life.

Kasbah du Toubkal is enchanting, comfortable, and authentic with a 100% local Berber team extending the warmest hospitality. They operate consciously with most walking to work from their villages, have low energy and water consumption, minimal waste, and encourage guests to offset their travel carbon footprint. They employ freelance mountain guides and muleteers with mules to carry food, supplies, baggage and sometimes guests for 15 minutes up to the retreat. They pay a fair wage and support local suppliers and shops, and 5% of Kasbah's turnover support local initiatives with a Village Association to preserve the environment with improve rubbish disposal, support mule welfare and vulture research, and not-for-profit projects in health, welfare and education for girls through the NGO Education For All which believes that 'an educated girl educates the next generation'.

Das Kasbah du Toubkal mit seiner spektakulären Lage im Hohen Atlas im gleichnamigen Nationalpark in Zentralmarokko ist ein beschauliches Hideaway, eingebettet in das Bergdorf Imlil mit Panoramablick auf fruchtbare Täler und den Jbel Toubkal, Nordafrikas höchsten Gipfel. Einst eine Festungsruine, wurde die "Altstadt" von zwei begeisterten Brüdern – Mike und Chris McHugo – mit der Langzeitvision restauriert, bis 1990 ein zukunftsfähiges Tourismusprojekt in einer fragilen Bergwelt mit lokalen Händen und Materialien zu entwickeln. Ihre inspirierendes Schaffensmotto besteht darin, Lebensqualität, Stolz und Lebenskraft der Einheimischen zu stärken und Auszeitsuchenden ein authentisches, immersives Reiseerlebnis durch Rückverbindung mit der Natur zu bieten. En passant gewinnen die Besucher Einblicke in die Umgebung des Atlasgebirges und erhalten die Lebensart der Berber.

Das Kasbah du Toubkal ist bezaubernd, angenehm und authentisch dank eines 100% lokalen Teams aus Berbern, deren Gastfreundschaft aus tiefstem Herzen kommt. Die Mitarbeiter gehen bewusst zu Fuß von ihren Dörfern zur Arbeit, verbrauchen wenig Energie und Wasser, produzieren kaum Abfall und motivieren damit Gäste, ihren CO_2-Fußabdruck zu kompensieren. Die EcoLodge beschäftigt freiberufliche Bergführer und Maultiertreiber, um Lebensmittel, Vorräte, Gepäck und manchmal auch Gäste die 15 Minuten hoch zum Retreat zu bringen. Die Hotelangestellten werden fair bezahlt und auch lokale Lieferanten und Geschäfte erhalten gute Konditionen. Fünf Prozent des Umsatzes fließen über einen Dorfverband in örtliche Initiativen wie umweltschonende Müllentsorgung, Maultierwohl, Geierforschung und gemeinnützige Gesundheitsprojekte. Unterstützt wird auch das Wohl für Mädchen durch Bildung. Die NGO Education For All glaubt, dass „ein gebildetes Mädchen die nächste Generation erzieht".

Traditional Berber kitchen. Page 162: Chris McHugo, Education For All boarding house with students, and hand woven Berber carpet sellers.

Page 158-161: The terrace area and interior dining room and hammam. Spectacular view from Kasbah du Toubkal.

Traditionelle Berberküche. Seite 162: Chris McHugo, das Internat "Bildung für alle" mit Schülern, Verkäufer von handgewebten Berberteppichen.

Seite 158-161: Terrasse, der Speisesaal und der Innenbereich des Hammam. Spektakuläre Aussicht vom Kasbah du Toubkal.

MANOR HOUSES, PORTUGAL

A Manor Home Away From Home

Built during the period of great wealth in Portugal, when trade followed the famous Portuguese discoverers who were the first to sail to America, Brazil, South Africa and Asia, the Manor Houses – rural palaces, quintas, solares and casas – can be found in beautiful and fertile areas in the regions of Minho and Douro in Northern Portugal. Most remained in the same family for many centuries, and nowadays, the owners offer travelers a unique and personalized accommodation, the warm hospitality of a family home, and an immersive experience of the manor's history and culture, the region's traditions and way of life, and the surrounding environment.

The Palace of Calheiros (Paço de Calheiros in Portuguese) has been home to the Calheiros family since 1450, standing proudly on a hill overlooking the verdant Lima valley, and surrounded by historic gardens, fruit trees, vineyards that produce the Vinho Verde Loureiro wine. The visionary Count Francisco Calheiros leads a dedicated team to welcome guests and share their history, customs and traditions. The wide range of activities includes traditional cooking lessons, nature walks, painting workshops, wine tasting, and spa rejuvenation. As part of the Solares de Portugal network, the operators are committed to the sustainable development of their community, the natural environment and tourism and see themselves as a pioneering source of inspiration. They prioritise the local community when hiring employees, folk dancers and workers during harvest season, and support local suppliers. They use renewable energy and enable wastewater to be treated, reused and forwarded to a pond reservoir to support biodiversity. Moreover, they organize Eco Circuit events in the community to create awareness of good environmental practices.

In der Zeit des großen Reichtums in Portugal erbaut, als im Zuge der portugiesischen Konquista der Handel mit Amerika, Brasilien, Südafrika und Asien zu florieren begann, warten heute die Casas Nobres und Solares do Portugal – palastähnliche Landsitze und Quintas – in den schönen, fruchtbaren Gebieten von Minho und Douro in Nordportugal auf. Die meisten Herrenhäuser blieben über Jahrhunderte hinweg in derselben Familie. Heute bieten die Eigentümer Urlaubern eine einzigartige, persönliche Unterkunft, die herzliche Gastlichkeit eines Familienanwesens und ein Eintauchen in Geschichte und Kultur, Traditionen und Lebensart der Region und der näheren Umgebung.

Der Paço de Calheiros ("Palast der Calheiros") ist seit 1450 Wohnsitz der Familie Calheiros und thront stolz auf einem Hügel mit Blick auf das grüne Lima-Tal, umgeben von historischen Gärten, Obstbäumen und Weingütern, die den Vinho Verde Loureiro produzieren. Der visionäre Graf Francisco Calheiros leitet ein engagiertes Team, um Gäste willkommen zu heißen und ihnen Geschichte, Bräuche und Traditionen näherzubringen. Zum vielfältigen Angebot gehören traditionelle Kochkurse, Naturwanderungen, Malworkshops, Weinproben und Verjüngungskuren im Spa. Als Teil des Netzwerks Solares de Portugal haben sich die Betreiber der nachhaltigen Entwicklung ihrer Ortsgemeinde, der Natur und des Tourismus verschrieben und verstehen sich als wegweisende Inspirationsquelle. Für den Hotelbetrieb werden vorzugsweise Locals eingestellt. Ebenso werden Volkstänzer und Erntehelfer aus der Umgebung angeheuert und lokale Lieferanten unterstützt. Durch Nutzung erneuerbarer Energien und Wiederverwendung aufbereiteten Abwassers für die Landwirtschaft über die Wasserspeicherung in Erdteichen kann Biodiversität erhalten werden. Zudem finden Ökorundgänge in der Ortsgemeinde statt, um Einheimische für vorbildliches Umweltengagement zu sensibilisieren.

The magnificent Paço de Calheiros can be seen from afar, standing among the vineyards atop a small hill. The view from the manor is of a carefully tended garden in the French baroque style, the passion fruit pergola and orangery, and the vineyards of the surrounding Minho region.

Schon von weitem ist das prächtige Paço de Calheiros zu sehen, das inmitten der Weinberge auf einer kleinen Anhöhe steht. Vom Herrenhaus aus blickt man auf einen sorgfältig gepflegten Garten im französischen Barockstil, auf die Passionsfrucht-Pergola und die Orangerie sowie auf die Weinberge der umliegenden Region Minho.

Casa do Barreiro in Ponte de Lima was built in 1652. It has a timeless central courtyard and idyllic gardens with painted tin-glazed ceramic tilework called Azulejos by the famous Portuguese artist Jorge Colaço on walls, fountains, and corridors of the house.

Das Casa do Barreiro in Ponte de Lima wurde 1652 erbaut. Es verfügt über einen zentralen Innenhof von zeitloser Schönheit und idyllische Gärten mit bemalten, glasierten Keramikfliesen des berühmten portugiesischen Künstlers Jorge Colaço, die Azulejos genannt werden an Wänden, Brunnen und in den Gängen des Hauses zu sehen sind.

Quinta do Monteverde is a 17th century manor house and walled estate between the countryside and the sea. The manor combines tradition with comfort and rooms have antique furniture and lovingly refurbished décor details carefully kept from generation to generation.

Quinta do Monteverde ist ein Herrenhaus aus dem 17. Jahrhundert. Das ummauerte Anwesen, zwischen Meer und Hinterland gelegen, verbindet Tradition mit Komfort. Die Zimmer sind mit antiken Möbeln ausgestattet und liebevoll renoviert, wobei die Details der Einrichtung von Generation zu Generation beibehalten wurden.

FINCA SERENA, SPAIN

Life In A Serene Farm

Majorca is a captivating island with rugged mountains and coastline, sandy beaches, open green spaces, and rustic country life. At its heart, the 40-hectare estate of Finca Serena offers a calming and exclusive retreat with a spa, an orchard, a vineyard, and a lush Mediterranean garden with ancient trees surround a 13th century farmhouse and rooms with earthy stonework, vibrant crimson bougainvillea and a relaxed and soothing nature-inspired interior.

A passionate owner – Pau Guardans – leads an dynamic team, committed to sustainability that is authentic and holistic. Finca Serena is wonderfully rooted to their local community and a regenerative farming culture, proudly show-cases local artisanal products and crafts onsite and has a circular approach to the consumption of water and raw materials. They support local suppliers and artisans, hire 80% locally, regenerate disappearing grape varieties, and biannually team up with individuals with Down syndrome to clean paths. They arrange guest experiences that surprise, engage with local artisans and suppliers, promote wellbeing with bountiful nature that nourish from farm-to-table-to-farm on site and from nearby farms. Guests are invited to join immersive and delightful experiences in the organic orchard, and during the annual vineyard harvest when they can roll up their sleeves, pick grapes, and make wine.

Finca Serena supports the Sustainable Majorca ambition and matches each Euro 'eco tax' charged to guests to help finance projects aimed at protecting the environment, restoring cultural heritage, and promoting eco-tourism on the island.

Mallorca ist eine faszinierende Insel mit schroffen Bergen und Küsten, Sandstränden, grünen Weiten und urigem Landleben. Inmitten dieser Insel bietet die Finca Serena auf 40 Hektar Grund ein besänftigendes, exklusives Retreat mit einem Spa, einer Obstplantage, einem Weinfeld und einem üppig mediterranen Garten. Das Gehöft aus dem 13. Jahrhundert, eingefasst von alten Bäumen, wartet mit Natursteinräumen und purpurrot blühenden Bougainvilleen auf und verwöhnt das Auge mit seinem entspannten, naturinspiriertes Wohlfühlinterieur.

Als passionierter Inhaber leitet Pau Guardans ein inspiriertes tatkräftiges Team, das auf authentische Art nachhaltig und ganzheitlich wirtschaftet. Die Finca Serena ist wunderbar mit dem Ort und dem regenerativen Landbau verwurzelt, präsentiert stolz lokale Manufakturerzeugnisse und Kunsthandwerk, verhält sich beim Wasser- und Rohstoffverbrauch ressourcenschonend und unterstützt lokale Lieferanten und Handwerker. Das Personal setzt sich zu 80% Prozent aus Einheimischen zusammen. Aussterbende Rebsorten werden neu gezüchtet, und alle zwei Jahre werden Menschen mit Downsyndrom in eine Wegesäuberungsaktion eingebunden. Die Finca arrangiert überraschende Experiences und fördert das Wohl der Urlaubenden mit Farm-to-Table-Angeboten der freigebigen Natur aus dem eigenen Garten oder von nahegelegenen Bauernhöfen. Die Gäste werden aufgefordert, ihre Ärmel hochzukrempeln und umfassende Erfahrungen zu machen, die Freude machen. So können sie z. B. im Bio-Obstgarten mithelfen oder bei der alljährlichen Weinlese Trauben pflücken oder Wein keltern.

Die Finca Serena unterstützt das Ziel "Nachhaltiges Mallorca" und lässt jeden Euro Umweltobulus in Projekte fließen, die dem Umweltschutz, der Restauration des kulturellen Erbes und der Förderung des Ökotourismus auf der Insel dienen.

The resort respected the original architecture. Rooms have views over the estate with its olive trees, open space, lush Mediterranean gardens, and trails.

Page: 178-179: Rooms are filled with natural light with an elegant and minimalist décor and natural cotton, linen, stone, wood and other local materials.

Unter Wahrung der ursprünglichen Architektur bieten die Zimmer einen Blick auf das Anwesen mit seinen Olivenbäumen, offenen Räumen, üppigen mediterranen Gärten und Wanderwegen.

Seite 178-179: Die Zimmer sind lichtdurchflutet und verfügen über eine elegante, minimalistische Einrichtung mit natürlicher Baumwolle, Leinen, Stein, Holz und anderen lokalen Materialien.

COQUILLADE PROVENCE RESORT & SPA, FRANCE

Inspirations Amidst The Vines

Coquillade Provence Resort & Spa is majestically perched on top of a hill, with a 360-degree panoramic view of Provence's landscape, in the middle of Luberon Regional Nature Park near Gargas France.

Its founder's vision combines luxury and respect for nature for a balanced way of life, and its inspired custodian GM – Alain Bachmann – and an energised team protect the authenticity and biodiversity of the surrounding nature and aim to be Climate Positive before 2030. Their vineyard AURETO became Climate Neutral in 2021 and aims to be Climate Positive in 2023.

Conservation efforts focus on forestland maintenance and humidifying its undergrowth to protect from fires and providing a refuge for wild fauna and flora. They purchase organic bathroom amenities and produce from local suppliers, and welcome gifts and recycled linen aprons from local artisans. They support "Pink October" fundraising for breast cancer, donate to cancer research, and provide hospital caregivers with free SPA access. To emit less carbon, geothermal energy powers the heating system, staff use electric club cars, and use bicycles or carpool to commute. Wasted food is fed to animals and a pyrolysis process burns bio-waste onsite and from neighbouring villages, to produce heat for the swimming pools and biochar residue is used to fertilise the soil.

Guests are invited to visit the vinification cellar to taste cuvées weekly and join the annual "culinary hike" and "village festival" to experience the local culture and winemaking traditions. A resident naturopath leads nutrition workshops, and hiking and biking tours are offered as well to create awareness of the environment and its biodiversity.

Das Coquillade Provence Resort & Spa thront majestätisch auf einem Hügel mit einem 360-Grad-Panoramablick auf die Landschaft der Provence inmitten des Regionalen Naturparks Luberon bei Gargas.

Die Vision seines Gründers verbindet Luxus mit Respekt vor der Natur für eine ausgewogene Lebensweise, und sein begeisterter Wächter, der Geschäftsführer Alain Bachmann, schützt zusammen mit einem dynamischen Team die Authentizität und Biodiversität der natürlichen Umgebung. Ihr gemeinsames Ziel ist es, noch vor 2030 klimapositiv zu sein. Ihr Weingut AURETO wurden 2021 klimaneutral, und sie wollen ihrerseits bis 2023 ebenfalls klimapositiv zu sein.

Der Naturschutz konzentriert sich auf die Waldpflege und den Erhalt der Feuchte im Unterholz zum Schutz vor Waldbränden, damit wildlebende Tiere und Pflanzen ungestört fortbestehen können. Bio-Pflegeprodukte werden lokal hergestellt und eingekauft, ebenso Willkommensgeschenke und recycelte Leinenschürzen. Sie unterstützen das Fundraising der Brustkrebs-Stiftung „Pink October", spenden für die Krebsforschung und bieten Krankenhaus-Pflegekräften kostenlosen Zugang zum Spa. Um weniger CO_2 auszustoßen, wird mit Geothermie geheizt, die Mitarbeiter nutzen Elektro-Clubautos und pendeln mit dem Fahrrad oder als Fahrgemeinschaft in die Arbeit. Weggeworfene Lebensmittel werden an Tiere verfüttert und Bioabfälle aus dem Ort und den Nachbardörfern werden durch Pyrolyse verbrannt, um mit der daraus gewonnenen Biokohle die Pools zu beheizen und den Boden zu düngen.

Die Gäste werden zur allwöchentlichen Verkostung der Cuvées in den Kelterungskeller und zur Teilnahme an der jährlichen „kulinarischen Wanderung" und dem „Dorffest" eingeladen, um die lokale Kultur und Weinbautraditionen zu erleben. Eine Heilpraktikerin leitet Ernährungsworkshops, und es werden auch Wander- und Radtouren angeboten, um die Gäste für Umwelt und Biodiversität zu sensibilisieren.

Surrounded by lavender, vineyards, olive trees and sun-baked walls, the resort is a place to unwind and practice self-care at the spa, snuggle in cosy and elegantly comfort, take the trails and explore the Luberon, or train for a triathlon under a sweeping blue sky.

Umgeben von Lavendel, Weinbergen, Olivenbäumen und sonnengebräunten Mauern ist das Resort ein Ort, an dem man sich entspannen und im Spa Selbstfürsorge betreiben kann. Sich gemütlich und elegant einkuscheln ist ebenso eine Option, wie auf Wanderungen den Luberon erkunden oder unter einem strahlend blauen Himmel für einen Triathlon zu trainieren.

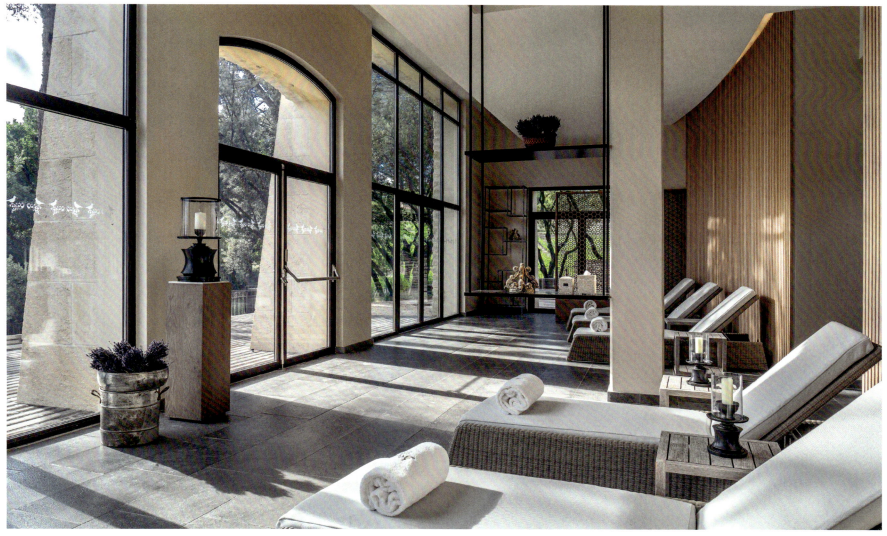

From their garden to table, guests can tuck into the full flavour of Provence.

Page 190-191: Restaurants offer creative menus for fine-dining in the Vaucluse region, fusion cuisine in the Luberon, or tapas in Gargas. Unwind and rejuvenate in a refined and relaxing spa.

Vom Garten frisch auf den Tisch, so können die Gäste den vollen Geschmack der Provence genießen.

Seite 190-191: Die Restaurants bieten kreative Menüs für Feinschmeckeressen aus der Vaucluse, Fusion aus dem Luberon oder Tapas aus Gargas. Schalten Sie ab und verjüngen Sie sich im luxuriösen und entspannenden Spa.

THE TORRIDON, SCOTLAND

Lochs, Munros And Bravehearts

Embracing a magnificent sea loch and majestic munros in Wester Ross on the West coast of Scotland, The Torridon is an exceptional 58 acres estate and hotel offering guests a sustainably luxurious escape and adventures that connect with Highland nature on mountains and at sea.

Operated by conscious second-generation owners and custodians – Dan and Rohaise Rose-Bristow – and their inspired team, they care about their community and the environment, and aim to become Climate Positive before 2030. They hire local staff, guides, and experts to provide livelihood and enhance the guest experience, support local suppliers and artisans, and allocates 5% of net profits to charitable donations. For conservation they action a forestry plan to harvest and plant new trees and support the UNESCO Wester Ross Biosphere. The Torridon Farm rears bonny Highland coos and Tamworth pigs, and the two-acre Kitchen Garden grows nourishing organic produce and invites residents in the community to explore. They lower their carbon footprint by using local timber chipped onsite to create biomass energy for heating, water is sourced from a bore hole includes drinking water that is bottled in reusable vessels onsite, all single-use plastics are eliminated and food waste is fed to coos and pigs and composted with grass, coffee grinds and shredding.

The Torridon aspires to be the finest hotel in Scotland that welcomes muddy boots! It is a place where visitors will feel delightfully special and enriched knowing that the positive impacts of their holiday will contribute to the sustainability of the community and the uniquely beautiful area to ensure it thrives for future generations.

Das Boutique-Resort Torridon ist ein außergewöhnliches 58 Hektar großes Landgut und Hotel an einem herrlichen Loch (See) und vor der herrlichen Kulisse majestätischer Munros (Berge) in Wester Ross an der Westküste Schottlands – ein luxuriöses Hideaway mit Nachhaltigkeitsethos und Erlebnissen, die mit der Natur des schottischen Hochlands zwischen Bergen und Meer verbinden.

Die selbstbewussten Inhaber – Dan und Rohaise Rose-Bristow – betreiben das Anwesen in zweiter Generation und kümmern sich mit ihrem begeisterten Team um ihre Ortsgemeinde und die Umwelt. Bis 2030 wollen sie klimapositiv sein. Mitarbeiter, Reiseleiter und Experten werden lokal angeworben, um Einheimischen ein Auskommen zu sichern und das Urlaubserlebnis für die Gäste zu fördern. Schottische Lieferanten und Handwerker werden getragen, 5 % des Nettogewinns gehen als Spende an Stiftungen. Naturschutzmaßnahmen umfassen ein Abholzungs- und Wiederaufforstungsprogramm und die Unterstützung des UNESCO-Biosphärenreservats Wester Ross. Die Torridon Farm züchtet wunderschöne Hochlandrinder und Tamworth-Schweine, und im zwei Hektar großen Küchengarten werden vitaminreiche Bio-Produkte angebaut. Auch externe Gäste aus der Umgebung dürfen das Anwesen erkunden. Mit selbst gehacktem Holz aus heimischen Wäldern wird Biomasse zum Heizen erzeugt und damit der CO_2-Fußabdruck verringert, Wasser (einschließlich Trinkwasser) wird aus einem Bohrbrunnen gepumpt und vor Ort in Mehrweggefäße abgefüllt, alle Einwegkunststoffe werden eliminiert. Die Lebensmittelabfälle werden an Hochlandrinder und Schweine verfüttert oder mit Gras, Kaffeesatz und Schredderholz kompostiert.

Das Torridon will das beste Hotel in Schottland sein, das Schlammstiefel willkommen heißt! Es ist ein Ort, an dem Besucher sich bereichert fühlen werden, weil sie wissen, dass sie durch ihren Urlaub der Ortsgemeinde Nachhaltigkeit bescheren und zum Erhalt einer einzigartig schönen Gegend beitragen – zum Wohl künftiger Generationen!

Torridon Farm rears highland cattle, Tamworth pigs and chickens, to be served in the restaurant 1887 and the Bo & Muc Brasserie.

Page 200-201: Lounges and rooms blend Scottish heritage with Victorian era features. Two acres of garden grow fruits and vegetables. The Whisky & Gin Bar offers 365 malts and 120 gins.

Die Torridon Farm züchtet Schottische Hochlandrinder, Tamworth-Schweine und Hühner, die im Restaurant 1887 und der Bo & Muc Brasserie serviert werden.

Seite 200-201: Lounges und Zimmer vereinen schottisches Erbe mit viktorianischen Elementen. Auf zwei Hektar Garten werden Obst und Gemüse angebaut. Die Whisky & Gin Bar bietet 365 Malts- und 120 Gin-Sorten an.

Arcturus Gin is handcrafted and locally foraged, a blended range of botanicals and pure Scottish Loch water. Owner Dan Rose-Bristow feels close to the land. Inspired chef Paul Green respects what the land grows and works within the season. Right side: The road leads to The Torridon.

Arcturus Gin wird in Handarbeit hergestellt und ist eine Mischung aus pflanzlichen Zutaten und reinem schottischen Quellwasser. Der Besitzer Dan Rose-Bristow fühlt sich dem Land sehr verbunden. Der kreative Küchenchef Paul Green respektiert, was das Land bietet und arbeitet mit saisonalen Zutaten. Rechte Seite: Die Anfahrt zum The Torridon.

WHATLEY MANOR, ENGLAND

Keep Calm And Gloriously Carry On

Less than 2 hours from London, Whatley Manor nestles within twelve acres of picturesque countryside on the edge of historic Malmsbury, in southern Cotswold's designated 'area of outstanding natural beauty'. Gracefully restored, guests are deliciously nurtured and calmly restored in this delightful 18th-century manor house, steeped in British tradition and sustainable luxury comforts.

Whatley's conscious and passionate GM – Sue Williams – and an inspired team embed sustainability in their culture, make learning hilariously fun, support communities, aim to be zero waste to landfill and Climate Positive before 2030. They hire locally when available, support local tradespersons and suppliers, initiate litter picks, invite senior citizens for garden tours, and promote traditional wool weavers and their craft. Key purchases gratifyingly give back, with Charity Water receiving 10% of bottled filtered water sales, purchased bicycles help a Sahel child get to school and buying teas gave work to refugees. A creative culinary team offers seasonal menus from 90% organic produce. They get their beef from farmer Tim next-door, source 60% of local ingredients within fifty miles, and sublimely turn citrus waste into vodka. To use less energy and water, all kitchen equipment is energy efficient, a biomass boiler supply energy to staff housing, and a garden bore hole supply its water needs. A garden team schooled in ecological horticulture gloriously restored the twenty-six gardens to their 1920's Arts and Crafts origins, grow organic ingredients, placed bat and bird boxes on twelve acres, and left some grounds undisturbed to help wildlife flourish all year round.

Weniger als zwei Stunden von London entfernt, liegt das Whatley Manor idyllisch eingebettet auf zwölf Hektar des malerischen Festlandes am Rande des historischen Malmesbury, im südlichen Cotswold, einem „Gebiet von außergewöhnlicher natürlicher Schönheit". In diesem anmutig restaurierten, bezaubernden Herrenhaus aus dem 18. Jahrhundert, das von britischer Tradition und nachhaltigem Luxuskomfort durchdrungen ist, können sich die Gäste kulinarisch verwöhnen lassen und sich in aller Ruhe erholen.

Sue Williams, die selbstbewusste und passionierte Geschäftsführerin von Whatley, und ein inspiriertes Team haben den Nachhaltigkeitsgedanken verinnerlicht und sorgen für viel Freude am Lernen. Sie unterstützen Ortsgemeinden, wollen bis 2030 ihr Null-Abfall-Ziel erreichen und klimapositiv sein. Sofern verfügbar, werden nur Einheimische eingestellt. Sie unterstützen lokale Handwerker und Lieferanten, initiieren Ramadama-Aktionen, laden ältere Bürger zu Gartenführungen ein und fördern das traditionelle Wollweberhandwerk. Wichtige Einkäufe geben erfreulicherweise etwas zurück: Charity Water erhielt 10 % aus abgefülltem Tafelwasser, einem Sahel-Kind kann mit einem Fahrrad für den Schulweg geholfen werden und Teekäufe verschufen Migranten Arbeit. Ein kreatives Küchenteam bietet saisonale Speisekarten mit 90% Bio-Produkten, kauft sein Rindfleisch bei Farmer Tim von nebenan und bezieht 60% der Zutaten aus der Region im Umkreis von 80 Kilometern. Zitrusabfälle werden auf vollendete Weise in Wodka verwandelt. Um weniger Energie und Wasser zu verbrauchen, sind alle Küchengeräte energieeffizient. Ein Biomassekessel versorgt die Personalunterkünfte mit Wärme, ein Bohrbrunnen deckt den Wasserbedarf. Das ökologisch geschulte Gärtnerteam hat die 26 Jugendstil-Gärten aus den 1920er-Jahren herrlich restauriert. Es wurden Fledermaus- und Vogelbrutkästen aufgestellt, damit sich die Tiere das ganze Jahr über auf 12 Hektar auf ungestörtem Terrain entwickeln können.

Executive chef Ricki Weston and his team curate a menu focused on the finest British ingredients and traditional cooking methods at Michelin starred restaurant - The Dining Room - and Grey's Brasserie. Head Gardener, David Pearce is an advocate of sustainable ecological horticulture.

Küchenchef Ricki Weston und sein Team kreieren im mit einem Michelin-Stern ausgezeichneten Restaurant The Dining Room und in Grey's Brasserie eine Speisekarte, die sich auf die besten britischen Zutaten und traditionelle Kochmethoden konzentriert. Der Chefgärtner David Pearce ist ein Verfechter des nachhaltigen ökologischen Gartenbaus.

HOTEL PALAFITTE, SWITZERLAND

Close To The Heart

On a platform surrounded by luminous reeds swaying in the wind, Hotel Palafitte (French for 'stilts') was built by Sandoz Family Foundation to showcase Swiss hospitality at its best, as part of the 2002 Swiss National Exhibition on Lake Neuchâtel. An intriguing arteplage themed 'Nature and Artifice' displayed manmade nature and probed issues of ecology, sustainability, and humankind's uneasy relationship with the planet; and a riveting Palais de l'Equilibre (French for 'Palace of Balance') wooden sphere onshore displayed timber's enduring potential as an economical renewable resource.

As the only remaining structure from Expo2002, Hotel Palafitte offers a wellbeing experience and a special gathering place for Neuchâtel's residents. It is close to the heart of the locally born and conscious GM – Pauline Laurent – who leads an inspired team committed to caring for their guests and doing more for their community and the environment. They hire local and support local suppliers when available. They organize events by the lake to promote artisans and participate in local charity events. To lessen their energy use and waste, they use renewable energy for electricity, have LED lighting, provide bathroom amenities from dispensers, grow herbs and compost food waste, and provide guest access to eBikes, eCar charges and transportation cards for Neuchâtel city. Surrounded by a soothing lake, vineyard landscapes, marshlands and bird sanctuaries, guests can find luxurious escape in calm nature, relaxed comfort and delicious wellness.

Auf einer Plattform, umgeben von leuchtendem, sich im Wind wiegendem Schilf, wurde das Hotel Palafitte (französisch für „Stelzen") von der Philanthropischen Familienstiftung Sandoz (FPFS) gebaut, um im Rahmen der Schweizerischen Landesausstellung 2002 am Lac de Neuchâtel die eidgenössische Gastlichkeit von ihrer besten Seite zu präsentieren. Eine faszinierende Arteplage mit dem Thema „Nature et Artifice" zeigte die künstlich gestaltete Natur und untersuchte Fragen der Ökologie, Nachhaltigkeit und der unbequemen Beziehung der Menschheit zum Planeten. Die hölzerne Kugel "Palais de l'Equilibre" („Palast des Gleichgewichts") stand sinnbildlich für die Unverwüstlichkeit von Holz als wirtschaftliche erneuerbare Ressource.

Als einziges verbliebenes Gebäude der Expo2002 bietet das Hotel Palafitte ein Wohlfühlerlebnis und einen besonderen Treffpunkt für Ortsansässige. Es ist das Herzensprojekt der gebürtigen Neuburgerin und selbstbewussten Geschäftsführerin Pauline Laurent und ihres begeisterten Teams, das sich ganz seinen Gästen widmet und sich für seine Ortsgemeinde und die Umwelt engagiert. Sofern verfügbar, werden Einheimische eingestellt und lokale Lieferanten bevorzugt. Sie organisieren Veranstaltungen am See, um das Kunsthandwerk zu fördern und nehmen an örtlichen Charity-Events teil. Für mehr Energieeffizienz und weniger Abfall nutzen sie erneuerbare Energien, sparen Strom mit LED-Beleuchtung und bringen Toilettenartikelspender an. Kräuter werden im hoteleigenen Gemüsegarten angebaut und Lebensmittelabfälle werden verkompostiert. Gäste erhalten E-Bikes und Zugang zu Ladestationen für Elektroautos sowie CityCards für den öffentlichen Nahverkehr in Neuchâtel. Umgeben von einem beschaulichen See, Weinbergen, Mooren und Vogelschutzgebieten finden Auszeitsuchende ein luxuriöses Hideaway in idyllischer Natur, entspannten Komfort und Wellness vom Feinsten.

A spectacular Lake Neuchatel can be viewed from the lake and shore pavilions built on stilts, meeting and event spaces, and The Bar, The Terrace and Restaurant 'La Table'. Hotel Palafitte offers its guests a haven of peace and a connection with serene nature.

Von allen auf Stelzen gebauten See- und Uferpavillons, den Tagungs- und Veranstaltungsräumen, der Bar, der Terrasse und dem Restaurant "La Table" hat man einen spektakulären Blick auf den Neuenburgersee. Das Hotel Palafitte bietet seinen Gästen eine Oase der Ruhe und der Verbindung mit der Natur.

BEAU RIVAGE PALACE, LAUSANNE, SWITZERLAND

Bringing Joy And Happiness

Since 1861, the magnificent and tranquil Beau-Rivage Palace overlooks the shores of Lake Geneva in Ouchy, Lausanne, Switzerland. It has witnessed defining moments in history and contributed to the destination's prestige, standing the test of time with tradition in motion and owners that care about the wellbeing of communities and the environment.

This luxurious and refined hotel has the most delightful purpose to bring joy and happiness to their guests and offer the finest in every experience. A conscious GM – Nathalie Seiler – works with a committed team and believes that the hotel and sister properties have a responsibility to lead and be Climate Positive. At a challenging time for the hospitality industry in need of reimagining service and reigniting career passions, she also believes that accountable sustainability and credible certification partners are key, and hoteliers must turn willingness into urgent action to help the planet and appeal to the new generation inspired by sustainable actions and companies with shared values.

The hotel is reducing its negative impacts and increasing their community support. They use renewable energy for electricity, have LED lighting, and use lake water to cool the building and heat the pool. Waste soaps are recycled, food waste is converted to energy, furniture and upholstery is repaired in-house, and Ipads replaced room directories and menus. Guests have access to eBikes and eCar charges and transportation cards for Lausanne city. They purchase and hire local when available, and they feel most inspired when supporting Planête Enfants Malades and Make a Wish Foundation and bringing a smile to the faces of parents and children.

Seit 1861 überblickt das prächtige, beschauliche Beau-Rivage Palace die Ufer des Genfersees in Ouchy bei Lausanne. Es hat geschichtsverändernde Momente erlebt und zum Prestige der Destination beigetragen, indem es den Zahn der Zeit mit nicht müde werdender Tradition überstanden hat, während die Eigentümern für das Wohl der Ortsgemeinden und der Umwelt sorgen.

Dieses luxuriöse, edle Hotel hat es sich zur Aufgabe gemacht, seinen Gästen Freude und Glück bringen und ihnen das Feinste vom Feinen zu bieten. Die selbstbewusste Geschäftsführerin Nathalie Seiler arbeitet mit einem engagierten Team zusammen und glaubt, dass das Hotel und seine Schwesterhotels die Verantwortung haben, eine Führungsrolle zu übernehmen und klimapositiv zu sein. In einer herausfordernden Zeit für das Hotel- & Gaststättengewerbe, in der Service neu gedacht und Karriereleidenschaft neu entfacht werden müssen, glaubt sie zudem, dass verantwortungsbewusste Nachhaltigkeit und glaubwürdige Zertifizierungspartner ganz zentral sind. Hoteliers müssen dringend zum Handeln motiviert werden, um dem Planeten zu helfen und die nachhaltigkeitsbegeisterte neue Generation durch Unternehmen mit gemeinsamen Werten anzusprechen.

Das Hotel reduziert seine negativen Auswirkungen und baut seine Unterstützung für das Gemeinwesen aus; dazu gehört die Nutzung erneuerbarer Energien, das Einsparen von Strom mit LED-Beleuchtung und die Gebäudekühlung bzw. das Beheizen ihrer Pools mit Seewasser. Weggeworfene Seifen werden recycelt, Lebensmittelabfälle werden in Energie umgewandelt, Möbel und Polster werden im eigenen Haus repariert, Raumverzeichnisse und Speisekarten werden durch iPads ersetzt. Gäste erhalten E-Bikes und Zugang zu Ladestationen für Elektroautos sowie CityCards für den öffentlichen Nahverkehr in Lausanne. Sofern möglich, wird vor Ort gekauft und geleast. Rundweg begeistert sind sie vor allem, wenn sie mit ihrer Unterstützung für Planête Enfants Malades und die Make-a-Wish-Stiftung ein Lächeln auf die Gesichter von Eltern und Kindern zaubern.

The luxurious Beau-Rivage Palace exudes serenity and history on ten acres of private gardens with a delightful display of animal and bird bronze sculptures and giant fruit installations. The rooms and suites are bright with natural light and terraces open to fresh air and a stunning view.

Das luxuriöse Beau-Rivage Palace strahlt Gelassenheit und Geschichte aus und liegt in einer zehn Hektar großen Parkanlage, die mit Tierskulpturen aus Bronze sowie riesigen Obstplastiken verziert ist. Die Zimmer und Suiten sind hell und lichtdurchflutet, und die Terrassen öffnen sich zur erfrischenden Seeluft und einer atemberaubenden Aussicht.

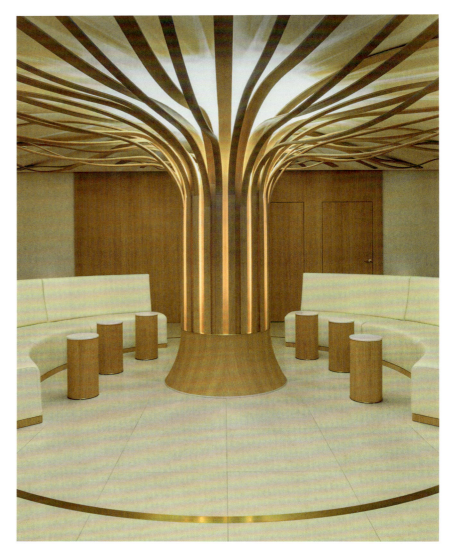

A magnificent Belle Epoque steamboat takes hotel guests on a cruise of Lake Geneva. The spa offers wellbeing treatments, rituals and naturopathy, and personalized fitness sessions. The garden includes a greenhouse to grow aromatic herbs and seven beehives to pollinate the flowers.

Ein prächtiges Dampfschiff aus der Belle Epoque nimmt die Hotelgäste mit auf eine Fahrt über den Genfer See. Das Spa bietet Wellness-Behandlungen, Naturheilkunde sowie personalisierte Fitness-Sessions. Der Garten umfasst ein Gewächshaus für den Anbau von Kräutern und sieben Bienenstöcke für die Bestäubung der rundum blühenden Blumen.

THE ALPINA GSTAAD, SWITZERLAND

The Last Paradise In A Crazy World

Authenticity meets Swiss sustainable luxury above Gstaad village at The Alpina Gstaad, a discreet and understatedly elegant alpine hotel and spa with spectacular views of the Bernese Alps. It is a secure and calm place, where discerning guests feel at home, relaxed by nature and alpine comfort, deliciously nourished and holistically restored, connected to their own rhythm and inner self, stimulated by cultural exchange, and enriched by art that evoke curiosity and emotions.

The Alpina believes that sustainability and luxury must go hand in hand and aims to become Climate Positive before 2030. It's a mindset and long-term process according to its Chairman and Creative Director Nachson Mimran. He credits their positive impacts to the hotel team who inspires others to consider it in their lives. Proud of their progress and keen to forge supportive partnerships, an inspired GM – Tim Weiland – and a motivated team ('the best ambassadors') action creative ideas, drive awareness and gain support from their stakeholders.

The hotel consciously reduce, reuse and recycle waste and renewable energies, use reclaimed energy from appliances to heat its pools and has beehive colonies to support biodiversity and cross pollination. They support local guides, tradespersons, suppliers, internships, and artwork creations concerned with environmental and social activism; sponsor mountain clean-up, youth sports events and classical music festivals; and engage specially challenged persons through paid work creation. Further away, the hotel funds support for people fleeing the war in Ukraine and collaborates with to.org to support mangrove afforestation projects for healthier ecosystems.

Hier trifft Authentizität auf nachhaltigen schweizerischen Luxus: Über dem gleichnamigen Dorf gelegen, lockt das Alpenhotel & Spa in seiner Diskretheit und dezenten Eleganz mit atemberaubenden Ausblicken auf die Berner Alpen. Es ist ein sicherer, ruhiger Ort, an dem sich anspruchsvolle Gäste wie zu Hause fühlen. Von der Natur und alpiner Gemütlichkeit umgeben, können sie sich hier bei feinstem Essen entspannen und ganzheitlich regenerieren, um sich mit ihrem eigenen Rhythmus und inneren Selbst zu verbinden, angeregt durch kulturellen Austausch und bereichert durch Kunst, die Neugierde und Emotionen weckt.

Das Alpina glaubt, dass Nachhaltigkeit und Luxus Hand in Hand gehen müssen, und das Luxushotel will noch vor 2030 klimapositiv werden. Es ist eine Denkweise und ein langfristiger Prozess, meint der Vorstand und Creative Director Nachson Mimran, der es dem positiven Einfluss seines Hotelteams zuschreibt, dass andere angeregt werden, ihren Lebensstil zu überdenken. Stolz auf ihre Fortschritte und bestrebt, unterstützende Partnerschaften zu schmieden, setzen Tim Weiland, ein begeisterter Geschäftsführer, und sein motiviertes Team („die besten Botschafter") kreative Ideen um, sensibilisieren ihre Gäste und gewinnen damit die Unterstützung ihrer Stakeholder.

Das Hotel setzt bewusst auf Abfallrecycling und erneuerbare Energien, verwendet rückgewonnene Energie zum Beheizen seiner Pools und hat eigene Bienenvölker, um die Artenvielfalt durch Fremdbestäubung zu fördern. Sie holen lokale Gästeführer, Händler und Lieferanten mit ins Boot und fördern Praktika und umwelt- und gesellschaftsbezogene Kunstwerke; zudem werden Bergsäuberungen, Jugendsportveranstaltungen und klassische Musikfestivals gesponsert. Besonders benachteiligte Personen werden durch bezahlte Arbeit inkludiert. Darüber hinaus leistet das Hotel Flüchtlingshilfe für Menschen aus der Ukraine und arbeitet im Rahmen von Mangroven-Aufforstungsprojekten zur Unterstützung gesünderer Ökosysteme mit to.org zusammen.

A discreet alpine getaway offering luxurious comfort, artistry and tradition. Three exceptional restaurants — Sommet, Megu and Swiss Stübli — are supervised by Michelin-starred Executive Chef Martin Göschel and offer authentic food, the finest products and attention to delicious detail.

Ein diskreter alpiner Rückzugsort mit luxuriösem Komfort, Kunst und Tradition. Drei außergewöhnliche Restaurants — Sommet, Megu und Swiss Stübli — bieten authentische Speisen und feinste Produkte mit viel Liebe zum Detail unter der Leitung des mit einem Michelin-Stern ausgezeichneten Küchenchefs Martin Göschel.

Winter at The Alpina Gstaad. Page 242-243: Spacious rooms and suites in classic Alpine style highlight the Saanenland's artisan heritage, tastefully enhanced with every modern comfort. Panorama Suite features a private outdoor jacuzzi. A spa oasis with a unique indoor swimming pool.

Winter im Alpina Gstaad. Seite 242-243: Großzügige Zimmer und Suiten im klassischen Alpenstil unterstreichen das handwerkliche Erbe des Saanenlandes, geschmackvoll ergänzt durch modernen Komfort. Die Panorama-Suite verfügt über einen privaten Whirlpool im Freien. Die Wellness-Oase glänzt mit einem einzigartigen Innenschwimmbad.

BERGHUUS RADONS, SWITZERLAND

Quiet Luxury Rules

In the canton of Graubünden, the Berghuus Radons awaits you at 2000 m above sea level with a view of the majestic Piz Forbesch above the Maiensäss-village of Radons. Its passionate owner and chef Fadri Arpagaus and local tradespeople lovingly restored the Berghuus into an intimate and comfortable 12 room retreat using local materials and opened in December 2020. Travellers appreciate the unique natural spectacles and glorious unagitated luxury – a tranquil stay full of rest and relaxation and without stress or anxiety.

Guests can delight in nature's seasonal spectacles in the mountains, valleys, and lakes where alpine flowers bloom in spring and summer, view marmot, ibex and alpine jackdaw, listen to roaring deers in the autumn, and enjoy starry nights in winter landscapes. There are wilderness tours with local guides and bike tours on miles of panoramic paths and off-road slopes.

Committed to sustainability, most energy used is renewable from hydro, drinking water is from a nearby well, and waste is recycled. In addition to local classics, international specialties are also served in the historic Arvenstube Ustereia. They purchase from neighboring farms, grow and produce herbs in the family's garden, air-dry their own ham and create Berghuus liqueurs from hand-picked pinecones. For food deliveries and guest transfer, they would like to build a gondola in the near future to replace motorized vehicles.

There are concerns about climate change and humans' growing consumption needs clashing with wildlife biodiversity. 2022's late winter snow, early spring ice melt and early summer heatwaves are affecting the Swiss glaciers. Wolves are a protected species until they attack livestock. Meanwhile, wolf presence is reduced by 15% each fall as part of a tightly controlled hunting season.

Im Kanton Graubünden wartet das Berghuus Radons auf 2000 m über dem Meeresspiegel mit einem Blick auf den majestätischen Piz Forbesch oberhalb des historischen Maiensässdörfchens Radons auf. Der passionierte Besitzer und Küchenchef Fadri Arpagaus und ortsansässige Handwerker haben das "Berghaus" mit lokalen Materialien liebevoll restauriert und zu einem urigen, komfortablen Hideaway mit 12 Zimmern umgebaut. Seit Eröffnung im Dezember 2020 bietet es allen, die einzigartiges Naturkino und herrlichen, bodenständigen Luxus schätzen, einen entspannten Aufenthalt, frei von Stress und Sorge. Die Gäste können sich durch alle Jahreszeiten hindurch an den Bergen, Tälern und Seen erfreuen, wo im Frühling und Sommer Alpenblumen blühen, Murmeltiere, Steinböcke und Alpendohlen beobachten, im Herbst den röhrenden Hirschen lauschen und im Winter sternenklare Nächte in verschneiter Landschaft genießen. Es gibt Wildnistouren mit Rangern und Radtouren auf kilometerlangen Panoramawegen und Trails abseits ausgewiesener Routen.

Der Nachhaltigkeit verpflichtet, wird die Energie hauptsächlich aus Wasserkraft gewonnen. Das Trinkwasser stammt aus einem nahe gelegenen Brunnen, Abfälle werden recycelt. Neben lokalen Klassikern kommen in der historischen Arvenstube Ustereia auch internationale Spezialitäten auf den Tisch. Die Zutaten werden bei benachbarten Bauernhöfen eingekauft, Kräuter und andere Erzeugnisse im Familiengarten angebaut. Das Berghuus stellt auch seinen eigenen luftgetrockneten Schinken her und brennt Schnäpse aus handverlesenen Fichtenzapfen. Für Lebensmittellieferungen und für den Gästetransfer wollen sie in naher Zukunft eine Gondelbahn bauen, um motorisierte Fahrzeuge zu ersetze. Es gibt Bedenken, dass mit dem Klimawandel und dem wachsenden Konsumbedarf der Menschen die Artenvielfalt drastisch abnimmt. Später Schneefall im Winter 2022, verfrühte Eisschmelze im Frühling und Hitzewellen im Frühsommer setzen den Schweizer Gletschern zu. Wölfe gehören zu den geschützten Arten, bis sie Nutztiere angriffen. Inzwischen wird die Wolfsdichte im Rahmen einer streng kontrollierten Jagdsaison jeden Herbst um 15% reduziert.

Bios

ALEXA POORTIER

Swiss resident Alexa Poortier is the founder of It Must Be NOW, an advisor and facilitator to hotels, tourism facilities and education institutions, to advance sustainability with accountability and transparency, support the Sustainable Development Goals and be Climate Positive. Her senior management experience spans over 35 years in hotels, PR and media in Asia Pacific, Europe, and Middle East.

Alexa believes that we all have a responsibility to act NOW to keep our planet healthy for future generations.

www.itmustbeNOW.com

Die in der Schweiz lebende Alexa Poortier ist die Gründerin von It Must Be NOW, einem Beratungsunternehmen, das Hotels, Tourismuseinrichtungen und Bildungsinstitutionen dabei unterstützt Nachhaltigkeit mit Verantwortlichkeit und Transparenz zu verbinden sowie Ziele für nachhaltige Entwicklung festzulegen und klimapositiv zu sein. Sie verfügt über mehr als 35 Jahre Erfahrung im Hotelwesen und PR im asiatisch-pazifischen Raum, in Europa und im Nahen Osten.

Alexa glaubt, dass wir alle die Verantwortung haben, JETZT zu handeln, um unseren Planeten für künftige Generationen zu erhalten.

www.itmustbeNOW.com

RETO GUNTLI

Swiss photographer Reto Guntli travels all continents for hotel shoots and magazine reportages on architecture, art, interior design, people and travel. As an accomplished photographer of luxurious lifestyle, he has produced over 50 books with teNeues, Taschen, Assouline and Thames & Hudson, and provides photography brand assets to top hotel groups and independent properties with co-photographer Agi Simoes.

They care deeply about the planet and are knowledgeable about sustainability.

www.retoguntli.com

Der Schweizer Fotograf Reto Guntli bereist alle Kontinente für Hotel-Shootings und Magazin-Reportagen über Architektur, Kunst, Inneneinrichtung, Menschen und Reisen. Als versierter Fotograf von luxuriösem Lifestyle hat er mehr als 50 Bücher für teNeues, Taschen, Assouline und Thames & Hudson produziert und liefert zusammen mit seinem Co-Fotografen Agi Simoes fotografische Markenwerte für führende Hotelgruppen und unabhängige Häuser.

Ihnen liegt der Planet am Herzen und sie kennen sich mit dem Thema Nachhaltigkeit aus

www.retoguntli.com

AGI SIMOES

Swiss resident Agi Simoes is internationally known for his lifestyle photography. He has worked on books for teNeues LIVING IN PARIS and LUXURY LIVING NEW YORK, and on dozens of books with other publishers in Europe, the USA, Asia and his native Brazil. He often collaborates with Reto Guntli and as a team, they contribute to international magazines such as AD, Elle Decor, Conde Nast Traveller.

Agi believes that sustainability is crucial to the preservation of the human race!

www.agisimoes.com

Der in der Schweiz lebende Agi Simoes ist international für seine Lifestyle-Fotografie bekannt. Er hat bei teNeues LIVING IN PARIS und LUXURY LIVING NEW YORK mitherausgebracht sowie an Dutzenden von Büchern für andere Verlage in Europa, den USA, Asien und in seiner Heimat Brasilien gearbeitet. Er arbeitet häufig mit Reto Guntli zusammen, und als Team leisten sie Beiträge für internationale Zeitschriften wie AD, Elle Decor und Conde Nast Traveller.

Agi ist der Meinung, dass Nachhaltigkeit für den Erhalt der Menschheit entscheidend ist!

www.agisimoes.com

Sustainability Alliance, Programs And Certification

NOW Force for Good Alliance is a consortium of extraordinary hospitality companies and tourism facilities that takes responsibility for their total impacts on communities and the environment, supports the UN Sustainable Development Goals and aims to be Climate Positive with accountability and transparency.

EarthCheck is the world's leading scientific benchmarking, certification (EarthCheck Evaluate, EarthCheck Certified and EarthCheck Eco Certified) and advisory group for travel and tourism.

The hotels, resorts and retreats listed below have committed to sustainability with accountability and transparency by joining the following alliance and certification program:

Die NOW Force for Good Alliance ist ein Zusammenschluss außergewöhnlicher Unternehmen aus dem Gastgewerbe, die Verantwortung für ihre gesamten Auswirkungen auf die Menschen und die Umwelt übernehmen, die Ziele für nachhaltige Entwicklung unterstützen und sich durch Rechenschaftspflicht und Transparenz für die Umwelt einsetzen.

EarthCheck ist die weltweit führende wissenschaftliche Benchmarking-, Zertifizierungs- (EarthCheck Evaluate, EarthCheck Certified und EarthCheck Eco Certified) und Beratungsgruppe für Reisen und Tourismus.

Die folgenden Hotels, Resorts und Retreats haben sich zu Nachhaltigkeit mit Rechenschaftspflicht und Transparenz verpflichtet, indem sie sich dem folgenden Bündnis und Zertifizierungsprogramm angeschlossen haben:

- Soneva in Thailand and Maldives: NOW Force for Good Alliance and EarthCheck Evaluate
- Joali Being, Maldives: EarthCheck Certified
- Four Season Landaa Giraavaru, Maldives: NOW Force for Good Alliance and EarthCheck Certified
- The Datai, Malaysia: EarthCheck Eco Certified
- The Legian Seminyak, Bali, Indonesia: NOW Force for Good Alliance and EarthCheck Evaluate
- Genghis Khan Retreat: NOW Force for Good Alliance and EarthCheck Evaluate
- Kasbah du Toubkal, Morocco: NOW Force for Good Alliance and EarthCheck Evaluate
- Coquillade Provence Resort & Spa: NOW Force for Good Alliance and EarthCheck Evaluate
- The Torridon, UK: NOW Force for Good Alliance and Earth Check Evaluate
- Whatley Manor, UK: NOW Force for Good Alliance and EarthCheck Certified
- The Alpina Gstaad, Switzerland: NOW Force for Good Alliance and EarthCheck Certified

Other: Finca Serena in Mallorca joined BioSphere in early 2022.

Other: Bawa Reserve in Indonesia is part of the World Wildlife Fund Indonesia's Signing Blue Program.

Imprint

© 2022 teNeues Verlag GmbH
All rights reserved.

Text: Alexa Poortier
Photos: Reto Guntli & Agi Simoes
Image & layout consultant: Reto Guntli

Editorial Coordination by Conrad Gminder & Birthe Vogelmann, teNeues Verlag
Production by Alwine Krebber, teNeues Verlag
Photo Editing, Color Separation by Jens Grundei, teNeues Verlag
Design by Anika Lethen
Translation (introduction & chapters) by Karin Weidlich

ISBN: 978-3-96171-386-8
Library of Congress Number: 2022944874
Printed in Slovakia by Neografia

Picture and text rights reserved for all countries. No part of this publication may be reproduced in any manner whatsoever.

While we strive for utmost precision in every detail, we cannot be held responsible for any inaccuracies, neither for any subsequent loss or damage arising.

Every effort has been made by the publisher to contact holders of copyright to obtain permission to reproduce copyrighted material. However, if any permissions have been inadvertently overlooked, teNeues Publishing Group will be pleased to make the necessary and reasonable arrangements at the first opportunity.

Bibliographic information published by the Deutsche Nationalbibliothek: The Deutsche Nationalbibliothek lists this publication in the Deutsche Nationalbibliografie; detailed bibliographic data are available on the Internet at dnb.dnb.de.

Published by teNeues Publishing Group

teNeues Verlag GmbH
Ohmstraße 8a
86199 Augsburg, Germany

Düsseldorf Office
Waldenburger Str. 13
41564 Kaarst, Germany
Email: books@teneues.com

Augsburg/Munich Office
Ohmstraße 8a
86199 Augsburg, Germany
Email: books@teneues.com

Berlin Office
Lietzenburger Str. 53
10719 Berlin, Germany
Email: books@teneues.com

Press Department
Email: presse@teneues.com

teNeues Publishing Company
350 Seventh Avenue, Suite 301, New York, NY 10001, USA

www.teneues.com

teNeues Publishing Group
Augsburg/München
Berlin
Düsseldorf
London
New York